Communio

Communio

Church and Papacy
in Early Christianity

LUDWIG HERTLING, S.J.

Translated with an Introduction by
JARED WICKS, S.J.

LOYOLA UNIVERSITY PRESS
Chicago   60657

LIBRARY OF CONGRESS
CATALOGING IN PUBLICATION DATA

Hertling, Ludwig, Freiherr von, 1892-
  Communio: church and papacy in early Christianity.
  Originally appeared in German in *Miscellanea historiae pontificiae*, v. 7,
1943; present translation was made from a later German version, "Com-
munio und primat," issued in the *Una sancta*, v. 17, 1962.
  Includes bibliographical references.

  1. Church history—Primitive and early church.
  2. Papacy—History.   I. Title.

BR166.H47   281'. 1   75-38777

ISBN 0-8294-0212-8

INTRODUCTION

ECCLESIOLOGY, as a distinct area of theological reflection, is a relatively recent phenomenon in the history of Christian thought. In fact, the earliest treatises concentrating systematically on the structure and mission of the Church were James of Viterbo's *De Regimine Christiano* (1301) and Juan Torquemada's *Summa de Ecclesia* (about 1450). Before that time, theological treatments of the Church were subordinate parts of Christology or sacramental teaching. Augustine wrote his most extensive ecclesiology within the framework of his theology of history in *The City of God*.

Especially in the earliest Christian centuries, we find only scattered attempts to present a theological vision of what the Church is and how its respective elements fit into a single differentiated unity. The closest we come to a patristic ecclesiology is St. Cyprian's argumentative work on the episcopate, *De Unitate Ecclesiae*. But there was in these early centuries a far more comprehensive "lived ecclesiology." An understanding of what it meant to be the church of Jesus Christ was implicit in the experience of professing the faith, worshiping together, and striving to live out the demands of Christianity in ancient society.

This implicit or lived ecclesiology of the first Christian centuries is the subject of the present essay by Ludwig Hertling, S.J. As he unfolds for us the rich notion of *communio*, we come to grasp from a distance something of the patristic experience of the Church. The first half of the essay describes the evidence found in inscriptions and letters and draws out what is implicit in a series of early Christian customs and stories. This material helps sharpen our gaze for the plurality of local churches, with each local church having a concrete, sacramental unity (*communio*) through the Eucharist and through the person of its bishop. The second half of Hertling's essay expands the peculiar notion of pastoral authority implied in *communio* and shows how the bishop of the local church of Rome served as the focal point of the network of churches linked together in the catholic, or universal, *communio*.

Ludwig Hertling is an Austrian Jesuit who taught at the Gregorian University. An earlier form of his essay on *communio* appeared in German in 1943 (*Miscellanea Historiae Pontificiae*, Volume 7). The present translation has been made from a later German version in *Una Sancta* (Volume 17, 1962). The translator has added seven explanatory notes to aid students who may not be familiar with certain terms and incidents of early Christian history which Hertling mentions in his text.

2

Obviously much has transpired in early Christian studies since Hertling first wrote on *communio*. One topic of further development concerns the early recognition of the Roman church as the normative master link in the chain of *communio* between the several local churches. Hertling sees this early form of the Roman primacy clearly attested in the second-century texts of Ignatius of Antioch and Irenaeus. Today, we have become more aware of the difficulties and ambiguities encountered in the interpretation of these texts. See, for instance, the study by James F. McCue, "The Roman Primacy in the Second Century and the Problem of the Development of Dogma," *Theological Studies* 25 (1964), 161-96.

On the other hand, an historical treatment of the emerging Roman primacy would take more account today of the positive archaeological evidence that the grave of Peter the Apostle has been found beneath the Vatican basilica bearing his name. Edgar R. Smothers reported on these finds in "The Bones of St. Peter," *Theological Studies* 27 (1966), 79-88.

Hertling's descriptive account of the relations between the bishops of the several churches focuses especially on the situation documented in the sources from the fourth century onward. Today, there are a host of newer studies that delineate the genesis of the episcopal structure as it emerged in the critical years during and immediately after the composition of New Testament documents like the Acts of the Apostles and the Epistles to Timothy and Titus. See, for example, Hans von Campenhausen, *Ecclesiastical Authority and Spiritual Power in the Church of the First*

3

Three Centuries (Stanford University Press, 1969); James A. Mohler, *The Origin and Evolution of the Priesthood* (Alba House, 1970); and Raymond Brown, *Priest and Bishop* (Paulist Press, 1970). But in spite of the fact that Hertling's work can be supplemented by newer historical studies, his relevance is by no means diminished.

RENEWAL OF ECCLESIOLOGY

Hertling has made a seminal contribution to the development of ecclesiology in our time. The Lutheran theologian, Werner Elert, has developed the close interrelation of sacramental sharing and the reality of the Church in *Eucharist and Church Fellowship in the First Four Centuries* (Concordia, 1966). Catholic theologians, such as Yves Congar, M.-J. Le Guillou, Jerome Hamer, and Joseph Ratzinger, have taken up the theme of *communio* as a central motif for understanding the nature and structure of the Church. They have shown that the great issues of Christian unity, ministry, authority, and collegiality can be set in proper light only when they are related to the fundamental reality of the Church as a network of sacramentally focused local churches bound together ultimately by the mutual openness of their eucharistic celebrations.

In a number of key passages, the Second Vatican Council used the language of *communio* in speaking of church membership, the episcopal college, and the eminent role of the local church. In the Constitution on the Church, the bond of *communio* was added to the three traditional criteria of faith, sacraments, and ecclesiastical government in the account of "full incorporation" into the visible Church (n. 14). The collegial unity of the episcopate

4

is repeatedly described in terms of the "hierarchical communion" linking the bishops of the world with one another and with the pope, the bishop of the primatial see (nn. 21-23). In an idyllic chapter (n. 26), this same Constitution describes the ideal local church, where the initial ecclesial *communio* unfolds into a vital communitarian life of Christian witness, eucharistic worship, and growing holiness. Thus, the theme of sacramental-ecclesial *communio* is one of the key conceptions of the recent ecclesiological movement of Catholicism.

Previous to this shift in Catholic ecclesiology, the central sacramental dimension of the Church was overshadowed by juridical conceptions, such as the scholastic master idea of a *societas perfecta*. The papal primacy of jurisdiction so outweighed the episcopate that it was seldom realized that the Holy Father was a bishop and exercised his primacy from within the worldwide body of bishops. The local parish or diocese was seldom grasped as an authentic realization of the Church, but was seen as simply an administrative unit of the universal body of Roman Catholicism. Obviously such a juridical emphasis and such a degree of uniformity made impossible any rapprochement with the Orthodox churches of the East and cut off the possibility of dialogue with the separated churches of the Protestant West. Hertling's essay on *communio* shows how the historical investigation of the early Church yielded a counterpoise to these prevailing conceptions of pre-Vatican II Catholic ecclesiology.

In addition to describing a pivotal concept in the development of recent Catholic thought, Hertling's work provides data pertinent to a number of questions of more contemporary concern. We should ponder the image of the Church sketched by Hertling, for it throws light on areas of movement and debate in our own day.

Communio AND ECUMENISM

The image of the ancient Church can serve to clarify the goal of ecumenical activity. Hertling describes the ancient plurality of distinct local churches, each one of which was a genuine assembly of Christians united in faith and in the possibility of participation in the same Eucharist. But even today it remains true that the fundamental Christian events, such as our baptism, our hearing God's word, and our reception of the Eucharist, do take place in a specific local church. In such a church, under the pastoral leadership of a given bishop, we are incorporated into Christ and granted *koinonia* (communion) with our brothers and sisters in Christ.

For our own day, the critical insight is that the separated bodies or denominations in both the East and the West are in this sense churches or even networks of churches linked by *communio* with each other. This is obvious in the case of the Orthodox and the Anglican-Episcopal churches. The latter even style themselves "the Anglican Communion." The same or similar bonds unite the congregations, synods, and federations of the many Protestant bodies as well. In them, believing men and women are incorporated into Christ and linked together by a bond of *communio*.

The great gain afforded by the ecclesiology of *communio* becomes apparent when we ask what is the goal of Christian ecumenical efforts. Ecumenists are not striving for the eventual transfer of masses of Christians to some system of doctrine, worship, and church polity other than their own. The goal, rather, is the extension of bonds of *communio* between these churches now existing as separated communities of faith and worship.

Thus, the great ecumenical task for all the churches is not simply the development of more adroitness in reinterpreting past differences. Sensitivity toward one's separated Christian brethren is only a beginning. The main challenge is that of total ecclesial growth. Developments must take place in all aspects of our church life, in all churches. The commitment to ecumenism means striving toward the day on which churches can turn toward each other and in the light of faith perform a mutual and corporate act of ecclesial recognition. This is the Christian unity we seek: churches acknowledging each other as valid articulations of what it means to be the church of Jesus Christ. Then the bond of *communio* can be extended between the bodies which have recognized in each other a total complex of genuinely Christian belief, worship, and polity. With full *communio* established, no further assimilation or organizational merger need be sought.

The image of the ancient Church that Hertling describes should keep us from conceiving ecumenism on a political model. The issues are not diplomacy, negotiation, and compromise. These must give way to realities of the sacramental sphere. For mutual ecclesial recognition is but the prelude to forging the bond of *communio* through unrestricted celebration of common Eucharists. Ultimately it is the eucharistic body of Christ that will make us into one body of Christ. This, however, will not be a single uniform and centralized organization, but a rich plurality of churches in full communion with each other.

Communio AND COLLEGIALITY

Hertling's work on church life in the patristic age opens an avenue for approaching the cluster of problems centered on episcopal collegiality. Vatican II has raised this to the level of a central tenet of Catholic ecclesiology. But the road to implementation of this new conviction has not been smooth. Ample evidence of this came amid the furor unleashed by Cardinal Suenens' interview of May 15, 1969. The whole discussion can now be reviewed in José de Broucker's *The Suenens Dossier* (Fides, 1970).

One reason for the stunted development of collegiality in practice may well be the way theologians have dealt with the doctrine taught by Vatican II. For instance, the influential German Catholic theologians, W. Bertrams, K. Mörsdorf, and K. Rahner, have exchanged arguments on the question whether after Vatican II one can say that the episcopate headed by the pope is in fact the "one subject of supreme authority" in the Church. Such a dispute is clearly guided by an ecclesiology that thinks of the universal Church before it considers the several local churches where bishops are found as chief pastors. It is a fact that this universalist view of the Church is the usual framework in which collegiality is defined, that is, as the responsibility the bishops share with the pope for teaching and policy-making in the universal Church.

For one steeped in the documents of the patristic age, this universalist mentality is too tinged with notions of absolute monarchy and uniform, centralized regulation of life.

8

This modern approach takes too little cognizance of the fundamental facts of life in the Church, especially the fact that bishops are first of all pastors of specific local churches. In his ministry, a bishop serves as the focal point of unity at the level where the church is repeatedly actualized in professing its faith and rendering dedicated worship to God. The first orientation of the bishop is toward promoting the Christian vitality of the people of a particular church.

The collegial aspect of the episcopal ministry is an important aspect of what a bishop brings to his people. Because he is a member of the worldwide college or order of bishops, his own people are related by *communio* to their fellow Christians of other, possibly quite diverse, churches. Because of his collegial union with the bishops of the world, a bishop can lift his people from the often stifling narrowness of a given locale or region. An Irish writer on the role of the bishop has expressed well this richer notion of collegiality:

> He is destined for the charge of a particular church, but it is precisely here that his role is collegial since it is through him and through his union with the college that this particular church is drawn into that wider communion of churches which constitute the one visible catholic Church. This is the real meaning of episcopal collegiality. Through their communion with one another the bishops symbolize and help to bring about the communion with one another of the several eucharistic communities over which they preside (Seamus Ryan, *Irish Theological Quarterly* 33 [1966], 31).

Thus, collegiality should refer less to a sharing in universal authority than to the concern and responsibility felt by bishops for the vitality and growth in Christian substance of the other churches of the world with whom they and their church are linked by bonds of communion.

This approach to collegiality from the vision of local churches in communion with one another gives impressive support to the proponents of decentralization and pluralism in Catholicism. Such a theological view does entail genuine authority for the pope, who is the bishop of the primatial church in the Catholic communion. But the ecclesiology of *communio* gives no support to the proponents and practitioners of regular curial supervision of the life of local churches. The strength and richness of the universal Church does not stem from uniformity and central control, but from the diversity and pluriformity of the many churches joined by the bond of communion.

Communio AND THE POPE'S ROLE

A major part of Hertling's essay describes how the patristic age saw the bishop of Rome functioning as the touchstone and criterion of the universal or catholic communion of the Church. To some, Hertling may even appear overly apologetic in arguing for an early functioning of the Roman primacy. But everyone should find illuminating his description of the concrete ways the Roman bishop contributed to the unity of the many local churches. One can well ponder the paradox that emerges: the basic function of the pope was not the performance of given official actions, but simply being present as the fundamental point of orientation and unity in the network of communion between the several churches.

10

This view of the papal office helps us today to cut through the panoply of titles and duties which the popes have amassed over the centuries. As Cardinal Suenens pointed out, we need not be greatly concerned that the pope is Primate of Italy, Patriarch of the West, and head of the Vatican State (*Suenens Dossier*, pages 31-33). His essential office is bishop of Rome, the primatial diocese of the Catholic world. As bishop of Rome the pope is in the episcopal college holding the first place among all the bishops. By being just this, the pope renders his primary and unique service to men and women of the Catholic communion. Through him we, with our bishops, are linked in communion to the vast number of Catholic Christians scattered over all the continents.

Of course this central ministry of unity has been further articulated over the centuries into a host of judicial and supervisory tasks that are often carried out by officials of the Roman curia. It is difficult to understand why local bishops were so often curtailed by this central bureaucracy. In our times we are seeing the first steps toward gradual decentralization. The view of the primacy sketched by Hertling both shows the ample justification for this in the Church's early tradition and lays bare the essential work of the pope as the nodal point of Catholic unity.

We live in a century that has seen repeated exercises of the papal teaching office, as in the dogmatic definition of our Lady's Assumption in 1950 and in an impressive series of encyclicals. Does the ecclesiology of *communio* throw light on this aspect of the pope's role in the Church? Does it offer any help in the debate over Hans Küng's attempt to substitute indefectibility in faith for infallibility in the solemn teaching of doctrine and morality (*Infallible? An Inquiry* [Doubleday, 1971])?

One of the first conclusions we derive from examining Hertling's historical evidence is that the pope must be concerned with what is being taught by the bishops with whom he is in communion. If *communio* is to be extended and to endure, the bishop of Rome must be satisfied that his brother bishops are proclaiming the authentic gospel of Christ to their people. The root of the papal teaching office appears to lie in this duty of discernment and evaluation that is the critical prelude to extending *communio*. Since this process of discernment is essential to the unity of the whole Church, one can expect the Holy Spirit to be granted to the pope in a special way to help him recognize the contours of the gospel in the various forms it will be proposed in churches throughout the world. This does not mean that the pope simply takes over the task of teaching in all the churches, nor that the bishops should be subjected to constant inquisitorial examination. But when crises and disputes arise, or when aspects of the gospel are languishing in oblivion, or when the bond of communion between churches is being threatened, then the papal responsibility would be called into play. Then the pope's peculiar charisma of discernment should be exercised in the service of unity for the Catholic communion.

Naturally, the pope's initial action must be brotherly dialogue with his fellow bishops who serve as chief pastors in the churches of the world. The great majority of recent papal encyclicals and apostolic letters have in fact been addressed to the bishops of the Catholic world. Modern popes

12

have thus acknowledged that their brother bishops bear the responsibility of pastoral teaching in their churches and dioceses. The logic of *communio* demands that bishops be both vigorous and sensitive in leading their people to deeper faith, to more intense eucharistic union with Christ, and to more generous service of people in need. The pope's charisma of discernment and his consequent duty to teach do not relieve the bishops of their responsibility of presiding in their own churches in a way that fosters the growth and Christian vitality of the people they serve.

Thus, the setting of the papal magisterium is clarified by an ecclesiology of *communio*. The pope teaches within, not over against, the collegial body of Catholic bishops. But in this interrelation of bishops and their churches, the critical issue is not the general fidelity of the Church to its mission or simply the lived loyalty of Christians to Christ. These *are* the ultimate questions, but the Church does not judge them in the public forum. The issue rather is the concrete, public proclamation of the gospel and the articulation of its implications for Christian living. The Church has a ministry of the Word of God to carry out, and one must ask whether the pope is an ultimately reliable judge in this area. This is a central question in the debate on infallibility. Hertling's data from the ancient Church implies that in a number of serious crises, such as Gnosticism, Montanism, and the rebaptism controversy, the bishop of Rome was respected as the one who could speak a decisive word of discernment and judgment on controverted teachings. The pope was an ultimate judge of what could be taught as Christian truth in the Catholic communion of churches.

This, of course, is not to say that the medieval and modern history of the papacy makes the claim to such a role luminously clear and attractively credible.

I am grateful to Professors Erwin Iserloh and Joseph Ratzinger for the introduction they gave in their Münster lectures to the ecclesiology of *communio*. New and valued stimulus has come from the latter's new book, *Das neue Volk Gottes* (Patmos, 1969). I want to thank Fathers Robert Murray and Philip Loretz, both Jesuits of Heythrop College, for providing a first draft of the translation, and Professor Ludwig Hertling for agreeing to this publication.

JARED WICKS, S.J.

Bellarmine School of Theology
Chicago, Illinois
July 1, 1971

14

Communio

CHURCH AND PAPACY

IN EARLY CHRISTIANITY

THE CONCEPT *communio*, in Greek *koinonia*, is one of the key ideas for understanding the early Church. It is one of those primitive concepts that contain a full range of ideas which are not yet reflectively developed. It was only much later that *communio* was analyzed and integrated into a theological system. When early Christians spoke of it they indicated at one and the same time a number of realities for which we now have different names.

This is not to say that *communio* was a vague or nebulous concept in early Christianity. People knew quite well what they meant by it. But for us it is not always easy to know which of its various meanings they intended to emphasize in a particular case. For this reason alone the ancient concept of *communio* has for us an ever-shifting richness of meaning.

Leaving aside, for the moment, questions about its biblical origin and later theological development, let us first attempt to define, or rather describe, what early Christians intended to say by the word *communio*. Its content could perhaps be best described in the following terms: *Communio* is the bond that united the bishops and the faithful, the bishops among themselves, and the faithful among themselves, a bond that was both effected and at the same time made manifest by eucharistic communion. *Communio* very often means simply the Church itself. St. Augustine says, "The Church consists in the *communio* of the whole world."[1]* Or, in another place, "I am in the Church, whose members are all those churches which, as we know from Holy Scripture, were founded and grew by the labor of the apostles. With God's help I will not desert their *communio* either in Africa or elsewhere."[2]

One who creates a new *communio* founds a new church. Optatus of Milevis states, "We [the Catholics of Africa] are in communion with the whole world and, in turn, the Catholics of all the provinces are in communion with us. But you [with the Donatists] have tried for a long time to establish two churches."[3]

Without entering here into the controversy over the original meaning of the article of the Creed which speaks of "the communion of saints,"[4] we can still say with certainty that for the Fathers the communion of saints very often simply meant the visible Church.

A synodal letter of Bishop Theophilus of Alexandria speaks of a certain Isidore, "who has been excommunicated

* Notes begin on page 77.

16

from the communion of saints by many bishops for a variety of reasons."[5] The Council of Nimes (394) speaks in its first canon of some Orientals who pass themselves off as priests or deacons but who are really Manichees: "They mark themselves with the 'communion of saints' by a pretense of commitment." The canon determines that such persons, if they were unable to show that they belong to the Church, should not be permitted to officiate at the altar.[6]

Union with the visible Church implies union with the invisible and triumphant Church, or rather the former union is the basis of the latter. As Nicetas of Remesiana put it in his exposition of the Creed, "after you have declared your faith in the Blessed Trinity, you attest your belief in the holy Catholic Church. What is the Church but the gathering of all the saints?" He then mentions the patriarchs, prophets, apostles, martyrs, and confessors of the past, present, and future.

> These form a single Church; they are sanctified by one faith and one way of life; they bear the seal of the one Spirit and have become one body. The head of this body is Christ, as Holy Scripture says . . . Therefore you believe that in this one Church you will attain to the communion of saints. Know that this is the one and only Catholic Church, established all over the earth, to whose communion you hold fast. There are other false churches, for example the church of the Manichees, but you must not have any dealings with these.[7]

Thus *communio* is the union of believers, the community of the faithful, and therefore the Church itself. This way of speaking is preserved even today in English, where "communion" can mean a specific community or denomination. For example, a Methodist will say of a Presbyterian, "He is not of my communion."

In order to understand the content of the concept *communio* among early Christians, a word study limited to the terms *communio* or *koinonia* will not suffice, because there are other words used to express the same thing. In Latin we often find *communio* replaced by *communicatio*, which had not yet acquired its modern meaning of "transmission of information." The Vulgate often translated the Greek *koinonia* by *communicatio*, as in Acts 2:42 (*communicatio fractionis panis*) and Philippians 1:5 (*communicatio vestra in evangelio Christi*). Thus in Second Corinthians 13:13 the Vulgate's *communicatio Spiritus Sancti* is not referring to the transmission of the Holy Spirit but to union with the Holy Spirit. In these passages the Greek has *koinonia*. The Vulgate also translates *koinonia* as *societas*, as in First Corinthians 1:9 (*vocati estis in societatem filii eius Jesu Christi*). However, the most common synonym for *communio* (*koinonia*) is *pax* (*eirene*). Often these two words are combined: *communio et pax, koinonia kai eirene*.

In modern languages, "peace" very often has the more negative meaning of absence of war, strife, attacks, and tribulation. So we say, "We want to live in peace," "Leave us in peace," or "World peace is endangered." Even when we speak of a peace treaty, we mean a mutual promise, subject to certain conditions, not to continue hostilities. A peace treaty is essentially a negative thing, whereas the positive counterpart would be a league or alliance.

But in the languages of antiquity, "peace" had a more positive meaning, often denoting some kind of union or alliance, as in the frequent Latin combination *foedera pacis*.

Obviously the word "peace" did not always have this meaning. When someone asked a visitor, "Do you come in peace?" he was asking whether his visitor had any hostile intentions. But when a man said good-bye to a guest with the words, "Go in peace," this could mean more than simply the promise not to hinder his leaving or the wish that he have a comfortable journey. It meant, most likely, "My good wishes go with you; let us remain bound in friendship." In the language of Christianity, "peace" is very common in the sense of fellowship, a bond of union, either in the combination "peace and communion" or simply as "peace." Tertullian wrote, "Heretics are not greeted in the peace and communion of the churches which go back to the apostles."[8] St. Augustine wrote to St. Jerome, "There has come to me a devout young man, a brother in Catholic peace."[9] By "Catholic peace," St. Augustine simply means to say that this young man is a member of the Church, a Catholic and not a heretic.

The most frequent formula occurring in inscriptions on early Christian tombs is "in peace." This phrase is found in various combinations: "He [She] rests in peace," "buried in peace," "lived in peace," "died in peace," or in the prayers, "May you live in peace," "Peace be to you with the saints," "Farewell in peace."[10] The formula "in peace" is so common and so exclusively Christian that it serves as direct and certain evidence for the Christian origin of a gravestone—a rule that we impress on students of epigraphy at the beginning of their studies.

Sometimes "in peace" can be interpreted in the modern sense as tranquillity or the absence of strife, as when we read on a tomb, "He sleeps in peace" or "Dear soul, rest well in peace."[11] This, however, does not hold for the most commonly occurring phrase, *depositus in pace*. Today, we might say, "With his burial, he has entered into everlasting peace," but we would never say, "He was buried in peace." Here, then, the phrase must mean something other than simply tranquillity or rest. This is all the more so when we read, "He lived in peace," or "He died in peace," or "He is to rise again in peace."[12] It is clear that here *pax* means "a community, the communion of saints," that is, the Church. *Vixit in pace* means that the person lived in the unity of the faith and of the sacraments of the Church. *Obiit in pace* means the same, namely, that he died in the community of the Church, or as we would say, "strengthened by the rites of the Church." *Resurrecturus in pace* means "he will live again in the communion of saints."

In this connection there is a very significant Roman inscription dated A.D. 357 which refers to a certain Quintianus who was buried "in rightful peace" (*in pace legitima*).[13] We know that in this year there was a schism in the church at Rome, during which the legitimate pope, Liberius, was opposed by an antipope, Felix II. Those who wrote on Quintianus' tomb the phrase, *in pace legitima*, meant to convey that he died as a member of the group which supported the true pope, not the antipope. They could just as well have written, *in communione legitima*. Admittedly, we do not know which of the two popes the relatives of Quintianus considered legitimate, but what is of interest is the way they simply referred to the *communio* of the Church as "peace."

On the mosaic pavement of a basilica discovered near Orleansville in Africa one can read the words, *Pax ecclesiae catholicae semper*.[14] This is not a prayer that the Catholic Church remain free from conflict, but is a greeting to those who enter the basilica, "May you ever be in the unity (or in the communion) of the Catholic Church."

Therefore *pax et communio (koinonia kai eirene)* are not two distant realities, but a single one expressed by two synonyms. Even today this manner of speech has been preserved in the form of address used in papal encyclicals when the pope is writing to the patriarchs, archbishops, and so forth, "who are in peace and communion with the Apostolic See." Here the pope does not mean that there is no dispute existing between himself and those named, but rather that he and they are united together by the bond of communion.

In Greek, *symphonia kai eirene* is also used instead of *koinonia kai eirene*. St. Athanasius writes that this *symphonia kai eirene* unites him with more than four hundred bishops.[15] It is true that in this context *symphonia* refers primarily to unanimity of opinion or to a common faith, but in combination with *eirene* it means something more. It is the same bond the Latins called *communio* or *pax*. Athanasius expressed the same concept in another passage by the phrase *koinonia kai agape*.[16] After the Synod of 340, Pope Julius had reassured him of "communion and charity," that is, ecclesial communion. Athanasius similarly speaks of Egyptian bishops who are united both among themselves and with himself in *agape kai eirene*.[17] Here also it is clear that *agape* does not simply refer to brotherly love, or still less to a love feast, but to the bond of *communio*. *Agape* is used by Ignatius of Antioch as a simple designation for a local church, as "the *agape* of the brethren at Troas."[18]

21

Therefore, we can say that all these expressions—*koinonia, eirene, agape, communio, communicatio, pax, societas,* and *unitas*—always signify the same reality of ecclesial unity, whether used alone or in combinations like *pax et communio* or *eirene kai agape.*

This bond of unity is more than sharing some identical attitude or having mutual friendly affection. Although the *communio* presupposes a common faith, this alone is not sufficient to constitute it. St. Ambrose wrote on behalf of the Council of Aquileia to the emperor about the admission (*impertienda communio*) of certain Oriental bishops. The difficulty was that the metropolitans of Alexandria and Antioch, "who have always been in unbroken communion with us" (*qui semper communionis nobiscum intemeratam habuere concordiam*), were opposing admission of these Orientals. "We, on the other hand, wish that they should if possible become part of our community." The orthodoxy of the petitioning bishops is therefore presupposed, but their admission to communion is not simply a question of orthodoxy: "it is a question of preserving intact the prerogatives of those who have long shared our communion, since we value greatly our good relations with them and, above all, because within the fellowship of the *communio* no cause for offense should be given."[19]

On the other hand, not every difference of opinion necessarily ruptures the *communio.* St. Cyprian wrote, "We know that some [bishops] do not wish to depart from something about which they are convinced and do not easily change their opinion. But, without breaking the bond of peace and concord with the other bishops, they neverthe-

22

less retain their own particular usages. In this matter we neither wish to restrict their liberty nor to lay down a law."[20] This text needs no explanation. The bond of peace and concord is the *communio*. The bishops of whom Cyprian speaks have clear differences of opinion among themselves, but this does not affect ecclesial unity. Hence this bond of *communio* must be something more than simply conformity in thinking.

In order to penetrate more deeply into the concept of *communio*, we must first of all consider how it is rooted in the Eucharist.

Communio AND THE EUCHARIST

Toward the middle of the second century, when Polycarp, bishop of Smyrna, came to Rome to discuss the dispute over the dating of Easter[21] with Pope Anicetus, the two bishops failed to reach an agreement. This, however, did not make them break the ecclesial unity existing between them. Irenaeus reported, "They still communicated one with the other."[22] By this he does not mean that they received the Eucharist from each other but, as he immediately adds, "in the assembly Anicetus charged Polycarp with consecrating [the Eucharist], and thus they parted from each other in peace."

In this case the sign of ecclesial unity consisted in the fact that, in spite of their difference of opinion and their failure to reach agreement, the bishop of Rome let the visiting bishop celebrate the Eucharist in his own community and in his presence. Obviously Polycarp gave Holy Communion to the clergy and the people of the Roman

23

church, just as the bishop of Rome was himself accustomed to do. From this fact all saw that the bond of ecclesial unity between the two bishops remained intact.

This incident is further illustrated by a passage from the third-century *Didascalia*. In it the bishop is given the following instruction concerning visiting clerics:

> If a bishop comes, let him sit with the bishop and be accorded the same honor as he receives. You, the bishop [of the place], should invite him to address your people . . . At the Eucharist he should speak the words. But if he politely defers to you, he should at least speak the words over the cup.[23]

We do not know whether this singular and for us quite strange ritual was ever actually practiced, since the *Didascalia* is a literary composition and not a liturgical book. The Greek redaction of the *Didascalia*, the *Apostolic Constitutions*, dating from the beginning of the fifth century, substitutes in this passage the words, "He should give the blessing (*eulogia*) to the people," which refer either to eucharistic communion or to the blessed bread which was given at that period as a substitute for communion. However this passage might ultimately be interpreted, it remains very important for our purpose, since it shows that ecclesial unity between two bishops was expressed in some form of joint offering or concelebration of the eucharistic sacrifice.

The letter of Irenaeus cited above mentions the custom followed by the bishop of Rome of sending the Eucharist to his priests as a sign of union.[24] This custom was still in force at the beginning of the fifth century. Pope Innocent I writes that at the Sunday liturgy the bishop of Rome sends the *fermentum* to the priests of the titular churches of the city. This consisted of consecrated particles sent for the express intention "that especially on this day they should not feel separated from fellowship with us."[25] Innocent goes on to say that this should only be done within the city, "because the 'mysteries' should not be carried too great a distance." This, therefore, is a meaningful rite, but not an essential one. In the cemetery churches outside the walls, the priests celebrate without the *fermentum*. At times, unconsecrated bread was sent over greater distances and was then used at the sacrifice of the Mass. St. Paulinus of Nola wrote to St. Augustine, "Please accept the bread that I am sending you as a sign of our union, and bless it."[26]

Since ecclesial unity found its expression in eucharistic communion, in times of schism the principle was followed that a person belonged to the group with whom he received communion. Macedonius, the heretical patriarch of Constantinople, forced the Catholics (and the Novatians) opposing him to receive the Eucharist from himself. He had their mouths forced open so that he could administer it to them in this manner.[27]

This conception was held for a long time. At the beginning of the seventh century, Sophronius tells of a Monophysite of Alexandria who would have liked to become a Catholic but was afraid of the other members of his sect. And so he received communion secretly in the Catholic basilica. The fact came to light, however, "and in this way his incorporation into the Catholic Church was brought about"[28]—something which we perhaps find somewhat oversimplified.

John Moschus, a contemporary of Sophronius, relates a similar incident. A certain lady wished to pray in the church of the Holy Sepulcher in Jerusalem, but the Mother of God appeared to her and forbade her to enter because she belonged to the Severian sect. "The lady immediately went in search of a Catholic deacon and when he came with the sacred cup, she received the holy body and precious blood of our great God and Savior Jesus Christ. So with no difficulty she became worthy to pray close to the holy and most precious sepulcher of our Lord."[29]

Sozomen tells a story about a married couple belonging to the Macedonian sect. The husband was converted to the true faith by a sermon of St. John Chrysostom and thereupon said to his wife, "If you do not participate in the divine mysteries with me (that is, receive communion in the Catholic Church), I will divorce you." The woman pretended to consent and at the liturgy Holy Communion was placed in her hand, as was then the custom. She bowed her head as if in profound adoration, but during this interval a servant girl secretly gave her the heretical Eucharist which she had instructed her to bring with her from their home.[30]

John Moschus introduces us to a monk of Cyprus who related that he was previously married and that both he and his wife belong to the Severian sect. One day he could not find his wife at home and was told that she had gone to the house of a neighbor to receive communion, as was still the custom in some places. The neighbor, however, was known to be a Catholic. The husband rushed over to stop his wife, but arrived just after she had received communion. So he took her by the throat and forced her to throw

26

up the consecrated particle which he then trod under foot. Two days later an evil spirit appeared to him and told him, "We are both condemned to suffer the same punishment." When asked who he was, the spirit replied, "I am the one who struck the Lord Jesus Christ during his passion."[31] John Moschus also tells of a Catholic stylite who prevailed upon a neighboring, heretical column-sitter to send him a consecrated host and then threw it together with a Catholic host into boiling water, whereupon the heretical host disintegrated, while the Catholic host remained intact.[32]

We are not concerned here with the historical reliability of such stories, nor with the rights or wrongs of what was done with the Eucharist, but with what they tell us about the understanding of sacramental communion in the early Church. The stories demonstrate, more clearly than any long theoretical discussion, how reception of the Eucharist was both the sign of and the means to ecclesial union. We could even say that it was the effective cause of incorporation into that unity. Naturally, in the early Church the individual's first incorporation was brought about by baptism, but thereafter this union was constantly consolidated through the Eucharist.

For this reason, Catholics who were obliged to travel in heretical countries carried their own Eucharist with them, a practice which Anastasius expressly approved at the end of the seventh century.[33] The heretics, on their part, did the same to avoid entering into communion with Catholics.[34] Because of this we can understand the report of Theodoret about the Messalians, a radical sect in Asia Minor. Their leaders did not think they needed to separate themselves from ecclesial union with the Catholics "because, according to them, the divine food is neither helpful nor harmful."[35] Today we would say that anyone who does not believe in the Blessed Sacrament separates himself from the Catholic Church. But the Messalians thought that since the Eucharist was nothing, no one is united to anyone else by means of it and therefore a man can receive communion wherever he wants.

An early fourth-century Gallic commentary on the Creed contains the following phrase, which would be incomprehensible except in the light of this understanding of the Eucharist: "The holy fellowship of the Father, the Son, and the Holy Spirit is the place where the faithful are bound to receive communion on Sundays."[36] This "holy fellowship" is simply the communion of saints, the true Church. The faithful are part of the true Church because in it they receive the Eucharist.

In this sense we can understand the worst accusation that St. Cyprian levels against a person in heresy or schism: "He is a rebel against the sacrifice of Christ, . . . he dares to set up another altar."[37]

Communio THROUGH LETTERS

Apart from the reception of the Eucharist, there was another sign of ecclesial unity that at first seems to be simply a matter of organization, but that was intimately connected with eucharistic communion and received its name from this, namely, letters of communion.

When a Christian, whether cleric or layman, set out on a journey—and travel was frequent in antiquity—he would first obtain from his bishop a document that served somewhat in the manner of a passport. These papers were called by various names: letters of communion, canonical letters, letters of recommendation,[38] or, more briefly, *formatae, tesserae,* or *symbola.* They were also called letters of peace (*pacificae* or *litterae pacis,* with *pax* being synonymous with *communio*). In 341 the eighth canon of the Synod of Antioch dealt with the right to grant such letters: "Country priests cannot grant canonical letters, but only letters of recommendation to neighboring bishops. Chorbishops,[39] on the other hand, can give letters of peace which are to be accepted by everyone."[40]

These Christian passports offered great advantages to travelers, since they had only to be presented and their holders would be received as brethren wherever they encountered other Christians. People bearing these letters would also be received as guests at the bishop's expense— a custom going back to the earliest times and mentioned in the *Didache.* This alone explains the remarkable frequency of correspondence between the bishops themselves. Every bishop could send messengers all over the Empire without incurring excessive expense.

When Julian the Apostate attempted to reorganize paganism on the same pattern as the Christian Church, he wished to introduce as well this system of letters. Sozomen wrote: "Especially he is said to have admired the letters by which bishops recommended travelers to one another, so that wherever they went and to whomever they came, they were always welcomed and entertained as friends on the evidence of these documents."[41] Thus these letters had considerable practical and economic importance, and they served as a valuable instrument for maintaining union between the bishops.

On one occasion, St. Augustine made use of this procedure to unmask a Donatist bishop in a public disputation. The Donatist was boasting that he was in no way separated from the true Church but was in communion with the whole Christian world. St. Augustine replied that this could be quickly tested. Could he (that is, the Donatist) give valid letters which would be accepted by the churches Augustine would name? Augustine began to list the ancient and venerable churches of apostolic foundation: Corinth, Alexandria, Ephesus, Antioch. It seems that the Donatist was unwilling to submit to this test, because everyone knew that his letters would not be accepted in any of these churches.[42]

The situation we have to imagine was something like this: every bishop, or at least those of any importance, in later times especially the metropolitan bishops, kept a list of the churches in the whole Christian world with which they were in communion. Such a list served as a register of the addresses to which letters of communion could be sent and from which letters were to be accepted. An incoming letter of communion was only valid if from a bishop whose name appeared on the list. The Donatist bishop in the dispute with Augustine was not on any lists except those of the Donatist bishops in Africa. St. Augustine could thus challenge him to issue a letter of communion addressed to the church at Alexandria or Antioch so as to test whether he was on the list kept by these orthodox and rightful bishops.

Naturally such lists had to be constantly revised and amplified. A notice of every bishop's death and of every new election had to be sent to all the other churches. Thus, in 251 Pope Cornelius not only notified the church of Carthage of his election, but also, as we happen to know, the church at Hadrumetum. Almost immediately the receipt of this notification was acknowledged from Hadrumetum, because the first Christian from there to arrive subsequently in Rome presented a letter of recommendation addressed to Bishop Cornelius. But meantime Novatian had also notified Carthage of his consecration as bishop of Rome and Cyprian, who was then bishop of Carthage, had suspended the entry of Cornelius on his list and had instructed the other bishops of Africa to do likewise. For this reason another traveler appeared at Rome from Hadrumetum with a letter which was not addressed to Cornelius but to the presbyters of the church of Rome—as though Rome was still a vacant see. At this, Cornelius sent an immediate protest to Cyprian.

Announcements of a death or of an election, and, in fact, ecclesiastical documents in general, had to be carried by clerics. The distance between Rome and Carthage was not so great as to prevent sending such a messenger on each occasion. Over greater distances, circular letters were sent, not to all the churches, but only to the principal ones, which in turn informed the neighboring churches. Sometimes, for greater safety, notification was sent simultaneously by different routes. Thus Dionysius of Alexandria notified Stephen of Rome that Fabius of Antioch was dead. This could mean either that the Antiochenes had notified him of the death of their bishop and requested him to inform Rome, or that to make doubly sure Alexandria was giving Rome direct additional notification. In the list of eastern bishops in communion with each other that Dionysius of Alexandria sent to Pope Stephen at Rome, there were notations beside the names of some to the effect that they were newly elected. In place of the deceased Alexander of Jerusalem, there is now a bishop called Mazabanes. Similarly, the titular of Laodicea is no longer Thelymides but Helidorus. Thus, in case they have not already been notified, Dionysius sought to inform the authorities at Rome that a succession had taken place in these sees so that the Roman list could be brought up-to-date.

It is solely in the light of this procedure that we can understand a frequently misinterpreted text of Tertullian dealing with events in the early days of Montanism. He wrote: "The bishop of Rome had already acknowledged the prophecies of Montanus, Prisca, and Maximilla, and accordingly was offering peace to the churches of Asia and Phrygia; but this man [Praxeas], by false statements about the prophets and their churches, and by insisting on the decisions of the bishop's predecessors, forced him both to recall the letters of peace already issued and to desist from his proposed approval of the spiritual gifts."[43]

The events that Tertullian described, in an obviously tendentious manner, were the following. The bishop of Rome, probably Zephyrinus (200-217), though he knew well enough that the prophetic movement of Montanus was flourishing in certain cities of Asia Minor, had not thought this to be sufficient reason for severing relationships with the bishops of that region and so had continued to issue letters of communion addressed to them. Possibly he had merely notified them of his election in the customary manner. This could be what Tertullian meant by the phrase, "was offering peace to the churches of Asia." That he had thereby either acknowledged or approved the prophecies of Montanus is Tertullian's own construction. In point of fact, decrees of approbation were not issued at that time, even by the see at Rome. By his attitude, the pope in question had done nothing more than demonstrate that he saw no sufficient reason for breaking off communion with the bishops concerned, of whom we do not even know whether they themselves had approved the prophecies of Montanus. Then, according to Tertullian, Praxeas had obliged the pope to recall his letters of peace. This does not mean that the pope had revoked a decree of approbation, but simply indicates that he had ordered that letters of peace should no longer be issued to these churches. Also, perhaps, he declared those already in circulation to be invalid. The statement that by invoking the authority of previous popes, Praxeas had forced the pope to adopt this measure may mean nothing more than that some previous bishop of Rome (Victor, Eleutherius, or most likely Soter) had already taken or at least threatened to take the same measures. Thus the whole incident is adequately explained by the procedures then current in a time well before the usages of decrees of approbation or of condemnation and in a time when there was no continual recourse to the bishop of Rome—which, in any case, is hardly to be expected in the early Church.

In times of crisis, especially when heresy or schism threatened, bishops would send to one another accurate lists of orthodox bishops for the purpose of control, even when there were no new successions to report. Thus Cyprian wrote to Cornelius, "I have sent you recently the names of the bishops appointed here [in Africa] who in full orthodoxy preside over the brethren of the Catholic Church . . . that you and our colleagues [in Italy] may know to whom you can write and from whom you can accept letters."[44] Similarly, Cornelius sent Fabius of Antioch a list of names and sees of all bishops who had joined in condemning Novatian.[45]

These official ecclesiastical letters were therefore a palpable and convenient sign of the union existing in the Church. At the end of the second century, Tertullian could write: "Thus all these great churches are a single Church, founded by the apostles, from which all of them are derived. They are all primitive, all apostolic, since they prove their unity in having among themselves the communion of peace, the title of brotherhood, and mutual certification of hospitality."[46] This *contesseratio hospitalitatis* as an expression of communion within the Church is not, therefore, an achievement of the third or fourth century, but dates from much earlier times.

It was therefore one of the main efforts of heretics, schismatics, or those excluded in some other way from communion, to obtain a *tessera* or letter of communion from one of the principal churches, preferably from Rome. On the strength of this they could hope to be once again accepted by the other bishops as well. Privatus of Lambesis, whom Cyprian called "the old heretic" and who had been excommunicated long before both by the bishop of Carthage and by Pope Fabian, took advantage of the vacancy of the Roman see after Fabian's death and tried to obtain a letter of communion for himself from the Roman clergy. Understandably, he had no success.[47] In the fourth century, St. Basil complained on one occasion that in Rome they granted letters of peace too easily to Orientals who in reality were not orthodox. This was a cause of embarrassment to the orthodox bishops of the East.[48]

Anyone whose name was on the list of only one of the principal churches was thereby in communion with all the other churches. Adopting the seven "angels" of the Apocalypse as a symbol for the universal Church, Optatus of Milevis wrote, "Whoever stands outside the seven churches is an alien. But if you have one of them, then through that one you are in communion with the other angels [bishops] and through the angels with the churches, . . . and through the churches with us."[49] In 375, St. Basil wrote to the faithful of Neocaesarea that their views and opinions should be in accord with the great number of bishops who were united over the whole world through the grace of God:

> Make inquiries of the Pisidians, Lycaonians, Isaurians, and Phrygians, of the neighboring Armenians, of the Macedonians, Greeks, Illyrians, Gauls, and peoples of Spain. Ask those in Italy, or the Sicilians, and Africans, those in the sound part of Egypt, and in the rest of Syria. Ask all of them who sends letters to us and who receives letters from us. From these letters you will be able to learn that we are all of one mind and hold the same views. Know then that one who rejects our communion separates himself from the whole Church. Think well, brethren, with whom you have communion. If you do not receive it from us, who will then recognize you?[50]

In the height of the Arian crisis, the same Basil complains, perhaps with some exaggeration, that the whole system of travel has come to a standstill in the Church and that bishops have no contacts outside their own cities, since almost no one knows whether his fellow bishops are still orthodox and, consequently, no one can send or accept letters of communion.[51]

Communio AND EXCOMMUNICATION

The necessary correlative of *communio* is excommunication. But we must not imagine that in the early Church excommunication was already totally identical with the vindictive and medicinal penalty of later canon law. For sometime it was simply the suspension of *communio*, that is, the severing of fellowship or the breaking off of ecclesiastical relations with another for some reason.

If a layman or even a cleric was guilty of a serious fault or misdemeanor, the bishop excommunicated him, that is, broke off relations with him and expelled him from his communion. The sinner who wished to reestablish relations and be readmitted to communion would accomplish this through the system of ecclesial penance. Here also we see that *communio* fundamentally referred to the Eucharist. Excommunication found its main expression in the sinner's exclusion from the Lord's table, and the lifting of excommunication was shown in his being once more permitted to receive the Eucharist.

The excommunication of an individual could be formally imposed, as in St. Cyprian's excommunication of Felicissimus or in the Roman bishop's treatment of the Gnostics Marcion, Cerdon, and Valentinus. But in the ma-

36

jority of cases, where the misdeed was well known, as with the *lapsi*[52] during times of persecution, excommunication was understood as automatic. Official steps were taken only when the question of readmission arose.

Upon occasion, bishops would break off relations with one another, as when there was suspicion of heresy. St. Basil acted in this way against his onetime friend, Eustathius of Sebaste. Basil was not his metropolitan, since Sebaste was itself the metropolitan see of Armenia, just as Caesarea was for Cappadocia. Thus Eustathius was in no way under Basil's jurisdiction.

In some circumstances, a layman or the people could break off communion with their own bishop. When serious charges were raised against John Chrysostom, bishop of Constantinople, the Emperor Arcadius refused to enter the church on Christmas Day and made it known to Chrysostom that he would not "communicate with him" until he had sufficiently cleared himself of the accusations.[53] Felicissimus, the layman mentioned above, had himself expressly broken off communion with St. Cyprian before the latter imposed excommunication on him.[54] Cyprian himself held that when a bishop was not orthodox, or not legitimately elected, the people had the duty of abstaining from communion with him.[55]

In these ruptures of fellowship, the essential issue is sharing in eucharistic communion. When the people broke off communion with their bishop, it meant that they no longer went to his church and no longer received the Eucharist from his hand. For this reason Macedonius attempted to compel his opponents by force to receive communion from his hands. After Novatian had become a schismatic, he made his adherents swear fidelity to him at the moment when he distributed the Eucharist to them.

Rupture of relations and the subsequent resumption of them both allowed of a certain gradation. Bishop Theophilus of Alexandria had excommunicated the archpresbyter Peter and the monk Isidore. The two traveled to Constantinople to lodge a complaint with John Chrysostom. The latter gave them an honorable welcome and allowed them to take part in the prayers of the community. They were thus permitted to take part in the liturgy, but they were not admitted to eucharistic communion until their case had been investigated.[56] John Chrysostom was then in communion with Theophilus of Alexandria. If he had simply admitted the two excommunicated men from Alexandria to full communion, this would have meant the rupture of relations with the bishop of that see. But because nothing against the two was known in Constantinople, since apparently no formal citation had been sent from Alexandria, Chrysostom saw no reason for treating these two otherwise respected persons as though they were fully excommunicated.

Such a gradation of excommunication was especially clear in Greek penitential practice, where we encounter the well-known degrees of penance in the works of Gregory Thaumaturgus as early as the third century. With the progressive completion of the prescribed penances, the penitent gradually drew nearer to the altar. The western church had similar degrees of penance without, however, such exact gradation as was the case in the East. But in the West we do find a gradation of kinds of excommunication practiced by the bishops among themselves. The "Statutes" of the Fifth Council of Carthage decreed regarding a specific case: "A bishop who has so acted should be separated from communion with other bishops and should content himself with communion with his own people."[57] In this way St. Augustine excommunicated the bishop of Fussala, whom he had himself consecrated.[58] In the same letter he mentions several analogous cases. St. Martin of Tours seems to have incurred such a mitigated excommunication because of his attitude during the trial of the Priscillianists, when he declared himself opposed to the execution of the heretics by the emperor. This punishment appears to have consisted principally in the exclusion of the bishop from the synod. This is much like the loss of active and passive voice—the right of voting and being elected—in modern canon law. We mention this procedure here because of the very significant way the early Church subsumed it under the concept of *communio* and excommunication.

On the other hand, the theoretical and theological aspects of exclusion from the Church remained very much undeveloped in the early centuries. At first, little thought was apparently given to the question whether and how far an excommunicated person still belonged to the Church. He was outside the Church and that was all there was to it. Only during the debates on the validity of heretical baptism in the time of St. Cyprian, and later during the Donatist controversy,[59] was the idea suggested that not all the separated persons were outside the Church in the same degree. St. Basil treats this in his letter to Amphilochius.[60] He distinguishes three degrees of separation: heresy, schism, and parasynagogism. Accordingly, heretics are totally separated, since they have only faith in God. In this group Basil names the Manichees, Marcionites, Montanists, and Valentinians, among whom baptism is judged to be not valid. Schismatics are those who have become separated as a result of ecclesiastical disputes or differences of doctrine which are capable of resolution, as regarding ecclesial penance (Basil is obviously thinking of the Novatians). Parasynagogists are priests, bishops, or unruly laity, who have joined together as an opposition party, as for example around a person removed from his position in the church because of some offense. Here someone refuses to submit to punishment and sets himself up as one holding authority and office. He subsequently acquires a few followers who together with him leave the Catholic Church. Basil thinks that if such persons eventually submit to penance they could even be restored to the ranks and offices they formerly held by reason of ordination.

Optatus is also of the opinion that the Donatists have not completely torn asunder the unity of the Church. Although there is division, the parts of the Church are in a certain sense still held together. The Donatists still have a Catholic way of life, and in spite of the human quarrel the sacraments remain the same.[61] The Donatist bishops are by their own wish no longer our colleagues, but they are nonetheless still our brothers.[62]

Earlier Tertullian sensed that there were different kinds of separation. Still, he could also say, "Heresies destroy unity no less than schisms and controversies."[63]

These passages show that the theoretical distinctions had still not been thought out. In the practice of the early centuries such distinctions were of little importance, since it was always left to the judgment of the bishop to decide

40

the manner in which a separated person was to be restored to communion.

But let us return to consider full excommunication. From our point of view, it is striking that nowhere in antiquity do we find a precise statement as to who had the right to excommunicate someone. Instead, it appears that everyone had this right—which, however, corresponds exactly with the early Christian conception of *communio*.

Each bishop could excommunicate another bishop, even if he were not his metropolitan or in any way his superior. But if subsequent events showed that the universal Church did not agree with the excommunication, then the separation recoiled upon the one who had first laid it down. He had not excluded the other bishop, but had shut himself out of communion with the others. This was the idea of Firmilian when he addressed Pope Stephen in the midst of the controversy over heretical baptism. "You have yourself committed the great sin in withdrawing from so great a community. Do not be deceived: you have separated yourself. For the true schismatic is the one who deserts the unity of the ecclesiastical community."[64]

For this reason, bishops would make strenuous efforts in times of crisis to prove that they were in communion with the largest possible number of other bishops all over the world. We recall how St. Basil listed almost all the countries of the world in his letter to the faithful of Neocaesarea. St. Athanasius did this in several passages of his writings, and Dionysius of Alexandria enumerated to Pope Stephen all the bishops in communion in the East, in order to show him that he should not with one act break off relations with so many churches. The conception at work here is not

41

simply that of majority rule, but rather that a bishop can effectively grant or refuse communion to another bishop only if the universal Church agrees with him.

Protagonists of church unity like St. Basil were greatly distressed when two bishops who were each in communion with a third bishop were themselves separated from one another. This state of affairs simply contradicted the concept of *communio*. St. Basil accuses the western bishops of being careless in granting communion to individual eastern bishops. Whether he did this rightly or wrongly in specific cases cannot be decided, but in any case it is certain that whenever he spoke of western bishops he actually meant the pope. Basil's charge was that they let themselves be won over simply by an orthodox profession of faith, with the result that they found themselves in communion with different people who were divided among themselves.[65] During the Antiochene schism this very thing happened to Basil himself. He was in communion with Meletius, while Athanasius and the bishop of Rome were in communion with the rival bishop Paulinus. But since Basil and Athanasius were themselves bound by deep ties, the situation was unbearable for Basil—especially since he could do nothing to remedy it.

Communio AND LOCAL CHURCHES

Individual local churches—comparable to the dioceses of today—constituted a *communio* in themselves. Admittedly bishop, clergy, and people formed a sort of hierarchical pyramid, but they were far more an organic unity. During the persecution of Decius, Cyprian wrote to his people from his hiding place that for the moment he wished

42

to make no decisions, since it had always been his principle to act only after consulting the clergy and seeking the consent of the people.[66] Regarding the reconciliation of the Roman confessors, Cornelius consulted the presbytery and also asked the opinion of the people. On the other hand, during a period when the see was vacant, the Roman presbyters wrote that the question of the *lapsi* would have to wait for an authoritative decision until a new bishop was elected.[67] These opposing strains of thought often make it difficult for us to understand specific situations in the early Church.

On one hand, there is no doubt that the bishop was the absolute and sole master of the house, on whom everything depended and through whose hands everything passed, even to details about the care of the poor. On the other hand, at the bishop's side we find the clergy, whom he addresses as his brothers, copresbyters, and codeacons, and without whom he decides nothing. Also the people themselves are expected to express their opinion on almost every question, even on the appointment of a lector.

From the outside, the local church seems like a single person. This is noticeable in the salutation of letters, as for example, "The church of God at Smyrna to the church of God at Philomelium and to the whole community of the holy Catholic Church in all places."[68] It is true that when the church of Smyrna used these words in reporting the martyrdom of its bishop, Polycarp, there was perhaps not yet a new bishop, but Philomelium was not a vacant see at the time. Ignatius of Antioch wrote his letters to the churches of Ephesus, of Smyrna, and so forth, addressing in them the whole community, and not just the laity alone.

Each of these communities had a bishop at the time, as in Smyrna where Polycarp was then bishop. Still, Ignatius wrote "to the Smyrneans." The church at Rome wrote to the church at Corinth near the end of the first century. We know from the testimony of Dionysius of Corinth that the letter was actually written by Clement, the bishop of Rome, who does not mention himself in the letter.

Sometimes bishops wrote in their own name and addressed their letter to the local bishop instead of to the community; nor is it always possible to assign the reason for the variation. The fact that Ignatius wrote in his own name and not as "the church at Antioch" may well be due to his being on a journey and quite far from Antioch. But Polycarp was not traveling when he wrote to the Philippians in his own name. Irenaeus seems to have written to Pope Victor, not "the church at Lyons" to "the church at Rome." Again, Dionysius of Alexandria wrote to Fabius of Antioch by name, but then in the letter he sometimes speaks to "my brothers" and then again to "my brother."[69] It makes little difference in the form or the content whether a bishop is writing in his own name or together with his church and in its name. Neither the tone nor the topic varies in Cyprian's letters, whether they end simply with his own signature or with his together with others, as in a synodal writing. Because of the *communio*, the bishop is neither the delegate nor the representative of his church, but in one sense he *is* the church. He can therefore address another bishop either as "my brothers" or as "my brother."

It is true that from the third century onward an individual bishop rarely writes as a church addressing another church. In part this stems from the fact that the more general letters of edification which could be read as part of the liturgy were no longer sent. Correspondence came to be restricted to concrete matters of business. But it would be wrong to conclude from this change in epistolary style to a change in the structure or organization of the Church.

As far as style is concerned, it must be remembered that the collective mode of thought and expression was used in ancient times in a manner quite foreign to us. In early times an ambassador or an orator addressed an entire state as "men of Athens" or "Romans." Treaties were also drawn up in this manner. The alliance and commercial agreement which the Romans made with the Carthaginians in 509 B.C. begins: "There is to be friendship between the Romans and their allies and the Carthaginians and their allies on these terms . . ."[70] A document of this sort permits no conclusions as to the political structure of the states in question—whether they had kings or consuls, or whether rule was monarchical, aristocratic, republican, or parliamentary. A letter described in First Maccabees 12:6 begins: "Jonathan the high priest, the elders of the nation, the priests, and the rest of the Jewish people, to the Spartans their brothers: Greetings." This is the reply to a previous letter which began: "Areios king of the Spartans, to Onias the high priest: Greetings" (First Maccabees 12:20). The point is that the address in the former letter, "to the Spartans their brothers," gives no indication that there was a king of Sparta at that time.

If modern church historians had taken account of such general considerations about the ancient world, they would have spared themselves a great deal of fruitless discussion about the origin of the monarchical episcopate. In point of fact, even in the earliest times we find no evidence in the sources for the existence of churches without an episcopacy. What we do find again and again—and in later centuries also—is the idea that bishop and church form a unit and are in one sense identical. The bishop is not simply placed over against clergy and faithful like a teacher over his pupils, a general over his soldiers, or a master over his servants. Even when such themes appear, they are accompanied by the more intimate relation of head and members. In fact, bishop and people are only thought of as separate factors in those abnormal situations in which head and members have come into conflict with one another.

The *communio* of individual local churches is also rooted in eucharistic communion. St. Ignatius wrote to the Philadelphians: "Be zealous to celebrate the one Eucharist. For the flesh of our Lord Jesus Christ is one, and he gives the one cup of his blood for our unity. There is one altar, just as there is one bishop with the presbyters and deacons, my fellow servants. [Keep this unity], so that what you do is done according to God."[71] And to the Ephesians: "Obey your bishop and presbyters, keeping free from any discord, breaking the one bread, which is the medicine of immortality and the antidote against death, giving eternal life in Jesus Christ."[72] And to the Smyrneans: "That only is the true Eucharist which is celebrated under the bishop or him whom he commissions. Where the bishop is, there the assembly should be, because where Christ Jesus is, there is the Catholic Church."[73]

From texts of this kind nothing can be deduced about the rite of eucharistic celebration. The instructions of the

Didache on the celebration of the Eucharist appear to be directed to all without distinction, as though all had the same function in the celebration. "As for the Eucharist, give your thanks in this manner. First, over the cup, 'We give you thanks, O our Father, . . . Then over the broken bread, . . . But no one shall eat or drink of your thanksgiving, but those who have been baptized with the name of the Lord."[74] If we had only this text from all of Christian antiquity, we might draw the conclusion that in these times there was no priesthood distinct from the community of the faithful and that all had the same function in the sacramental celebration. But in the light of the collective forms of speech, and especially of the collective way of understanding the local church, this difficulty disappears. The instruction is directed to the community, to the *communio* of clergy and faithful without specification of the detailed functions each had. True, we cannot deduce from such texts that the bishop alone had the power of consecration, but still less can we conclude that the laity possessed it.

Communio AND AUTHORITY

All that we have seen so far indicates that for the early Christians *communio* was a reality, a living institution, which existed independently of the willingness or intention of any single individual. It was a sacramental institution. The excommunication of the sinner consisted in his exclusion from the eucharistic communion, and his reincorporation into the *communio* took place by his readmission to the Eucharist. The letters of communion whereby church authorities testified that an individual belonged to the Catholic communion had for their immediate purpose his

47

admission to the Eucharist of another community. At the same time, *communio* had a juridical dimension inseparably connected with the sacramental aspect. Its juridical character is clear where ecclesiastical authority rules on incorporation or exclusion from communion, and when this authority issues letters of communion and decides whether similar letters from elsewhere are to be accepted or not.

Some modern critics wish to see in early Christianity nothing more than a multitude of autonomous bishops. Friedrich Heiler, commenting on Cyprian's understanding of the Church, wrote, "For Cyprian the unity of the episcopate is not guaranteed by a definite institution, but consists solely in the *concordia mutua* by which the individual bishops maintained brotherly relations among themselves. Cyprian's idea of the unity of the Church was well expressed by Caspar as 'union in charity between bishops and synodal groupings of equal standing.' "[75] We do not wish to go into Cyprian's theoretical notion of the Church, but it must be emphasized that the unifying element that bound the bishops—and therefore the entire Church—together was, even in Cyprian's time, something very different from mere agreement in attitude and a sense of brotherhood. Clearly, some differences of opinion did lead to severance of the bond of unity, but not all differences were of this kind. Although the unity of faith was one of the prerequisites for forming the bond of union, this bond could endure through differences on important questions. Brotherhood, as an affection arising from personal friendship, played a secondary role—for the simple reason that the majority of bishops did not know each other personally.

48

One might be tempted to see the unifying bond that held the Church together as a community of interests. The deputies of a particular party in a parliament, for example, are often not united by brotherly love nor even by complete uniformity of opinion. It can happen that they hold diverse views even on important issues. But they sacrifice their personal opinions for the sake of party solidarity. What unites them is still not a juridical bond, but the conviction that only by combined action can they maintain their influence on the government, realize specific points of their program, and keep their backing in the electorate united for the next election. Would not such a community of interest have been sufficient to hold together the bishops of the early Church without recourse to juridical ties?

Here again the answer can only be negative. For such a community of interests only arise when a group must show a united front against outsiders or when common action is called for. Amazingly, the early Church gives no evidence of such organized action. The history of the persecutions shows no indication that the bishops of the world ever joined hands in common defense even though, at least in the third century, their influence extended over a notable part of the population of the Empire. The bishops of the ancient Church do not even appear to have been interested in the expansion and growth of the Church through missionary action. The individual bishops in antiquity were not bound together by the conviction that they must stay together in order to achieve a particular goal, but by the conviction that their unity was already present as a given fact, independently of what any individual might think or feel or do. Thus we come back again to the sacramental-juridical bond of *communio*.

We find this unifying bond clearly displayed through the whole history of the ancient Church. One cannot even speak of its development, as if it were less extensive or less deeply sensed in the second than in the fourth or fifth century. At most there was development only in this, that in the course of time a certain casuistry emerged. Through practice—and less because of theoretical considerations—specific cases came to be recognized that led immediately to the rupture of communion, while others came to be understood as less serious. Gradually, the gradations of communion came to be recognized. At first there was only the simple alternative of communion or excommunication, but later some intermediate stages were found, such as exclusion from a synod without exclusion from the universal Church. A certain uniformity developed in the use of communion letters. At first these seem to have been simply letters of recommendation to another person or community, like St. Paul's Epistle to Philemon. Then they became official documents or passports, addressed to a bishop or to a group of bishops by name. The latter letters were more general in content, being confined, for example, to the statement that the bearer possessed the peace of the Roman church.

In time, more and more importance was attached to the lists of bishops, which were seen not simply as checklists for issuing and accepting communion letters, but as a controlling expression of the *communio* existing between bishops themselves. Finally, when letters of communion were no longer given, these lists survived as the two-leaved tablets cataloging the bishops in communion, from which one would read at the Memento of the Mass. Deleting a bishop's name from this list was then equivalent to severing communion.

In customs of this kind, modification or development did occur, although we cannot always specify the exact steps in such modifications. But the idea of *communio* was an enduring and living reality from the time St. Paul wrote to the Corinthians, "God is faithful, by whom you were called into the fellowship *(koinonia, communio)* of his son, Jesus Christ, our Lord" (First Corinthians 1:9), and "The cup of blessing which we bless, is it not a participation *(koinonia, communio)* in the blood of Christ? The bread which we break, is it not a participation *(koinonia, communio)* in the body of Christ?" (First Corinthians 10:16). Half a century later we find St. Ignatius of Antioch referring to the "one Eucharist" symbolizing the union between the bishop and the faithful. In the middle of the second century, Anicetus and Polycarp did not sever communion despite their difference of opinion. Instead they celebrated the Eucharist together as a sign of their unity. At the turn of the third century, Tertullian speaks of "the certification of hospitality" *(contesseratio hospitalitatis)*. In the third century, Cyprian called one who left the Church "a rebel against Christ's sacrifice," who "dared to set up another altar." Cyprian's letters are a rich source of references to the practice of communion letters. The chain of evidence continues on to the inscription, *Depositus in pace*, referring to burial in communion with the Church. Finally, there are the pious anecdotes reflecting the idea of *communio* held in the Byzantine age of the sixth and seventh centuries.

Through all of this there is no change in the basic notion of *communio*—nothing which heightens or diminishes it. And even today the Church prays over the gifts of bread and wine on the feast of Corpus Christi: "O Lord, graciously bestow upon your Church the gifts of unity and peace which are symbolized in this sacrifice we offer you."

Communio AND THE CHURCH OF ROME

The network of the *communio*, as we have seen it in Christian antiquity, appears at first to allow for no church to be subordinate or superior to any other church. In fact, in certain circumstances, each bishop could presume to express the will of the universal Church. Each bishop could excommunicate any other bishop and thereby separate him from universal communion. Within the *communio* all are equal. No one has rights or powers which the others do not possess in the same degree. At first sight, therefore, the system of *communio* seems to exclude any special prerogative for the see of Rome.

At the end of the second century we can observe the initial formation of metropolitan groupings among the bishops of the same civil province. The first traces of this are the synods that Victor of Rome called just before A.D. 200 in an attempt to settle the controversy over the celebration of Easter. On this occasion the future metropolitan sees made their appearance in some regions. By the fourth century, organized ecclesiastical provinces, as they were later called, were fully developed.

Historical studies treating this development, up to the institution of the patriarchates, invariably lead to the negative conclusion that the primacy of the Roman church was not a product of this process of organization. It was not the case that the hierarchy of the Church grew up like a pyramid, with the bishop of Rome at the apex over bishops, metropolitans, primates, and patriarchs. On the contrary, the overdevelopment of the metropolitan system actually obscured, for a while and to some extent, the prerogatives of the Roman see. Nonetheless, at least from the fifth or sixth century onward, these Roman prerogatives are an undeniable fact. Since they did not arise out of the metropolitan organizations, we must look elsewhere for their origin.

Was it actually true that the primitive conception of ecclesial *communio* left no place for the Roman primacy? We shall see that the ancient *communio* not only had a place for the Roman primacy, but that such a system itself led to the primacy of Rome by logical necessity.

For a bishop to show that he belonged to the *communio* of the Church, it was sufficient for him to be in communion with any other church of the *communio*. In a passage quoted above, Optatus of Milevis said, "If you have one of them, then through that one you are in communion with the other angels [bishops] and through the angels with the churches, . . . and through the churches with us."[76] Therefore it was sufficient if one was in communion with the bishop of Gubbio, or Calama, or Cyzicus; for if one of them belonged to the universal communion, through him one would be in communion with the whole Church. But if it became doubtful whether the bishop of Cyzicus belonged to the *communio*, communion with him was no longer of value. The bishop of Cyzicus must first show that he really belonged to the communion of the

53

whole Church. From this we see the practical need of a criterion by which one could discover whether an individual bishop belonged to the *communio* or not.

The simplest criterion was that of a large number of bishops. If one were in communion with hundreds of other bishops all over the world, then one's communion would be genuine, even if an individual bishop might refuse to grant communion. This impressive and easily understood criterion was often used, especially among the Greeks. St. Athanasius, St. Basil, and others, often reel off names from across the whole Roman Empire to show that they are in the true *communio* of the Church. No one asked precisely how many constituted a majority, since it was not a question of counting heads but simply of showing that one had an overwhelming majority.

Another criterion was union with the ancient churches founded by the apostles themselves. This criterion was often applied in Africa against the Donatists.[77] Since there were several hundred Donatist bishops in Africa in the fifth century, the criterion of the overwhelming majority was not so impressive. Augustine therefore challenged the Donatists to direct their reproaches not just against the bishop of Carthage or of Rome, "but also against the churches of Corinth, Galatia, Ephesus, Thessalonica, Colossae, and Philippi, to whom as you know, the Apostle Paul wrote; or against the church of Jerusalem where the Apostle James was the first bishop; or against that of Antioch, where the disciples were first called Christians."[78]

Such a criterion had already been employed by earlier ecclesiastical writers against Gnostics and other early heretics, when the issue was less the unity of the Church than

54

the inviolate character of the deposit of faith. Thus Irenaeus said, "When differences arise in any question, must we not have recourse to the most ancient churches where the apostles lived and learn from them a sure answer to the question at issue?"[79] And Tertullian wrote:

> It is clear that all teaching agreeing with that of the apostolic churches, from which the faith took its origin as from a mother, is to be judged true. For there can be no doubt that these churches received it from the apostles, the apostles from Christ, and Christ from God . . . We are in communion with the apostolic churches and our teaching must differ in no way from theirs. That is the testimony of truth.[80]

Such criteria were easily applicable in situations where a certain amount of information and agreement was shared by both sides. In such cases there was no need of recourse to an ultimate criterion and no need to explain just how a particular church over which there was no dispute had come to belong within the *communio*. But when such an ultimate explanation was given, one inevitably came to speak of communion with Rome.

Optatus wrote about the Roman bishopric, "Siricius succeeded Damasus and is now our colleague. Through him the whole world is one with us in the same *communio* through exchange of letters of communion."[81] Optatus speaks here of the *commercium formatorum*, which we described above, to make clear to the Donatists through this institution that the decisive list of bishops is the one kept by the Roman church. A church in communion with Rome is in communion with the whole Catholic Church. In principle, of course, this would be said of any rightful church, as Optatus himself said in the passage we cited about the "angels" of the churches. To prove membership in the universal *communio*, it was enough for a particular church to show it was in communion with some other church that in its turn was in communion with the others. This, of course, could begin a chain of demonstration—but this ended with *communio* with Rome. When Optatus wrote that through the church of Rome he was in communion with the whole world, he knew quite well that not a few churches were then not in communion with Rome. Still, he spoke of "the whole world." *Communio* with Rome was simply *the* communion and a church not sharing that communion was simply not acknowledged.

St. Augustine, in describing the time of Cyprian a century and a half earlier, wrote:

> [Carthage] had a bishop of no small authority, who had no need to fear having a great number of enemies, because he knew he was linked by letters of communion both with the Roman church, where the authority (*principatus*) of the Apostolic See always flourished, and with the other lands, from which the gospel had come to Africa.[82]

The same notion was expressed by Pope Boniface I (418-422), a contemporary of Augustine:

> The structure (*institutio*) of the universal Church took its origin from the honor given to Peter. All rule in the Church consists in this, that from Peter, as from a fountainhead, the discipline of the whole Church has been derived as this church grows and expands . . . It is certain that this church is related to the churches spread over the whole world as the head to its members. Whoever cuts

himself off from this church places himself outside the
Christian religion, since he no longer remains part of its
structure. I hear that certain bishops want to set aside the
apostolic constitution of the Church and are attempting to
introduce innovations against Christ's own commands.
They seek to separate themselves from communion with
the Apostolic See, or, more precisely, from its authority.[83]

The Protestant historian E. Caspar called this passage
the first concise statement of a vision of church structure
and development showing the characteristic papal stamp.[84]
But, in fact, the idea that the Roman church was the head
of the *communio* was widely held at this time and is much
older than the beginning of the fifth century.

In the year 381, St. Ambrose urged the Emperors Gratian and Valentinian to take steps "that the Roman church,
the head of the whole Roman world and the sacred apostolic faith, be not disturbed, since from it there goes forth
to all the others the rights of the treasured *communio*."[85]

After a long journey eastward, St. Jerome wrote to
Pope Damasus:

I address the successor of the fisherman and of the disciple of the cross. I want to follow no one but Christ and
therefore I am united in communion with your Holiness,
that is, with the see of Peter. I know that the Church is
built on this rock. Whoever eats of the Lamb outside this
house commits sacrilege.[86]

And he continues,

Having migrated because of my sins to this wilderness on
the border between Syria and lands outside civilization,
I am not able to receive the holy body of the Lord from
your Holiness. I attach myself here to your colleagues, the

57

Egyptian confessors . . . I have not met Vitalis, I reject Meletius, and I know nothing of Paulinus. He who does not gather with you, scatters; he who does not belong to Christ, belongs to the Antichrist.[87]

Jerome refers here to the schism then dividing the patriarchate of Antioch, in which he was living. He knew he was obliged to decide in favor of one of the three competing bishops, but he did not know how to resolve the problem of their conflicting claims. Therefore he simply affirms that he is in communion with Rome, which is the ultimate point at question.

These testimonies are clearly earlier than the time of Boniface I, but still from the fourth century. We have no need to suppose, however, that this conception emerged during this century. It was just as clear for Cyprian in the third century, who wrote to Pope Cornelius shortly after the latter's election that he was striving "to bring all our colleagues to recognize and hold to you and your communion, that is, to the unity and charity of the Catholic Church."[88] Here *communio* with the Roman bishop is identical with belonging to the Catholic Church. This identification (*communicationem tuam id est catholicae ecclesiae unitatem*) could not be made so simply regarding any other church, not even Alexandria or Carthage, even though Cyprian was well aware of the important place Carthage—and he himself as its bishop—occupied in the whole Church.

On another occasion Cyprian wrote to the same Cornelius with reference to the African schismatics: "Worst of all, they have elected a pseudo-bishop from among the heretics and they dare to set sail [for Rome] to approach the chair of Peter and the primary church from which is born (*exorta est*) the unity of the priesthood. They dare to bring this church letters from schismatics and sacrilegious people, not reflecting that even the Apostle Paul praised the faith of the Romans, among whom unbelief can make no entry."[89] When Cyprian speaks of the *unitas sacerdotalis*, he means the community of bishops, the *communio episcoporum*, which originates from Rome. He cannot have meant this historically, since Rome was not the first missionary center. Historically, the Church began from Jerusalem. Cyprian's *exorta est* must therefore be a present perfect, referring to the once-for-all and ever renewed origin from Rome of the *communio* linking the bishops. Rome is thus the focal point of the *communio*, not as the geographical center but as the center of its power and legitimacy.

The same conception emerges from Tertullian's account of the Montanists' separation from the Church. According to him, the decisive moment came when the bishop of Rome, under the influence of Praxeas, revoked the letters of communion that had been issued and perhaps already sent to the churches of Asia and Phrygia.[90] Tertullian's account may have been historically inaccurate, but the main thing, the principle, is clear: membership in the Church stands or falls through communion with Rome.

This is the *principalitas* of the Roman church spoken of by Irenaeus even before Tertullian. "With this church, because of its special preeminence, all the other churches must agree."[91] Obviously, the literal text here (*ad hanc ecclesiam convenire*) does not mean that all ought to go to Rome, but that they should be in accord with Rome, or—as we would now say—that they must be in communion with Rome. Perhaps Irenaeus' original Greek text had

59

koinonein where the Latin reads *convenire*. Granted that Irenaeus is speaking here of agreement in faith; still, this is itself one aspect of ecclesial *communio*. In any case, the meaning of the passage remains the same: Rome is the central church—or the center of the Church.[92]

We can also interpret in exactly the same sense the much-discussed words written by Ignatius of Antioch, the disciple of the apostles, about seventy years before Irenaeus. He called the church at Rome, "the one presiding in charity."[93] Some see here a metaphor which likens the Roman church to a bishop who presides at the celebration of the love feast, the agape of the early Church. Others would translate it as "president of the brotherhood of love." To us it seems more likely that *agape* is here simply a synonym for *koinonia* or *communio*. We saw how the language of early Christianity often joined *communio*, *koinonia*, *pax*, *eirene*, and *agape* in combination or used them interchangeably as synonyms. Thus Ignatius could well be referring to the same preeminence of the church at Rome that for Irenaeus was the normative focus of unity. Ignatius sees the Roman church presiding over the *communio* as the head and the center of its sacramental unity.

Even the pagans knew that a true Christian was one in communion with the bishop of Rome. When Paul of Samosata, bishop of Antioch, was deposed by a synod for heresy, he refused submission and would not hand over the church and the bishop's house to the new bishop. The case came before Emperor Aurelian (270-273) and, as Eusebius wrote, "He decided the case quite correctly, decreeing that the house was to be handed over to the one who receives letters from the head of the Christian religion in Italy and the bishop of Rome."[94]

The fact that Eusebius calls this decision "quite correct" is evidence for his understanding of the Church. This text is of special value since elsewhere in Eusebius there is practically no indication of how he conceived the Roman primacy. He frequently speaks of the bishops of Rome and even records the whole line of Roman episcopal succession, but the general impression is that he regarded Rome as simply one of the principal churches—no different from Antioch or Jerusalem. But the text on the emperor's decision raises the issue of the ultimate criterion of membership in the *communio*. Even though Antioch was an apostolic church and was in fact older than Rome, Eusebius says that it is "quite correct" to base the decision on communion with Rome.

When Athanasius was deposed by the Synod of Tyre in 355, he traveled to Rome to have Pope Julius confirm his communion with the Roman church. Bishop Marcellus of Ancyra did the same when he was deposed about the same time. Athanasius related that Julius and the bishops united with him "judged in our favor the question of the *communio* and bond of charity."[95] The verb used here (*kuroun*) refers to an authoritative confirmation. One could speak of Athanasius' action as the lodging of an appeal. But it is not precisely as if he went from one tribunal where he had lost his case to a higher court in search of an overruling. Instead, he wanted to have declared before the whole world that he was in communion with Rome and therefore that no one could convict him of crime. The verdict of the

61

Synod of Tyre was not simply overruled, but was shown to be impossible and ineffective from the start, which is something much more than a successful appeal to a higher court.

Especially the Christians of the eastern part of the Empire repeatedly emphasized their communion with Rome. Only this explains the remarkable convergence of eastern teachers of every kind in Rome, which is noticeable even in the second century. The list begins with Marcion, Cerdon, Valentinus, Heracleon, and other early Gnostics. Then came Hegesippus, Justin, and Tatian, who were succeeded by the elder and the younger Theodotus and their followers. Still later there were Proclus and Praxeas, and finally Origen himself. This point has been made often and there is no need to expand on it once again here. Some of these teachers came to Rome for purposes of study. Like Hegesippus and Origen, they wished to become familiar with the apostolic tradition of the Roman church. But most of them wanted to teach in Rome, even though the Christian community of Rome was not particularly favorable terrain for the complicated lectures and often exotic ideas propounded by these visitors from the East. Rome's attraction was simply that of the center of Christianity. *Communio* with Rome was for them of such great value that some, like Marcion and Valentinus, made strenuous efforts to maintain it in spite of repeated measures taken against them.

WHY THE FOCAL POINT IN ROME?

The fact that the Roman church held in some sense a privileged position in the early centuries is rarely contested today. In any case, it was the "first see" (*prima sedes*). Thus, the real question is what this undeniable primacy meant and how it is related to the later forms of papal primacy. So far we have sought to understand this primacy as the focal point of the *communio*. Before we tackle the question of the connection between this and the later papal primacy, we should examine briefly other elements in the early Church that could have led to the early emergence of Rome's preeminence.

One totally inadequate explanation is that the Roman primacy emerged from a chain of literary documents as proposed in the work of Erich Caspar.[96] In his reconstruction, the first step was Tertullian's phrase "every church which is akin to Peter" (*omnem ecclesiam Petri propinquam*),[97] by which the church of Rome was for the first time set in relation to Peter the Apostle. Cyprian then took the next step and was the first to designate the Roman see as chair of Peter.[98] He also applied the text of Matthew 16:18 for the first time to the church of Rome. Pope Stephen, in a stroke of genius, took over Cyprian's deduction and in the baptismal controversy[99] turned Cyprian's weapon against him. Caspar claims to find this documented in the letter of Firmilian, in which Firmilian is supposedly bewildered by the unexpected turn of events.[100] Although the rest of Christendom took no note of these maneuvers, Caspar sees these literary texts as responsible for firmly establishing the doctrine of the Roman primacy in the Church.

This explanation, however, is totally implausible. In an important critique of Caspar, Karl Adam pointedly observed:

> The great question which repeatedly arises with regard to Caspar's work is whether strict historical method allows the isolation of the earliest extant witnesses and defenders

of an explicit doctrine of the primacy from the streams of unreflected but very living faith in the Roman primacy. In this way, the first written evidence becomes not merely the theological interpretation of the faith, but actually the sole creator of the Church's doctrine of the primacy. Thus the doctrine itself comes to be presented as a merely literary product.[101]

In the Church, as elsewhere, theoretical formulations usually follow facts and events. Institutionalization is not the result of argumentation. Furthermore, in the Church it has always been extremely difficult to introduce radically new ideas without immediately arousing protests from all sides.

Another, historically far more plausible, explanation is that which derives the privileged position of Rome within the Church from the eminence of the city as capital of the Empire. The civil importance of a city was, from the beginning, a significant factor contributing to the prestige and significance of its episcopal see. But the fact that Rome was the imperial capital only explains why Rome was chosen as the center of the Church instead of Jerusalem, the original center, or some other city such as Antioch. Who made this choice, and who planned the transfer from Jerusalem to Rome, whether the apostles, or Peter and Paul, or Peter alone, is not important here. The point would simply be that the center was established at Rome consciously and deliberately because Rome was the capital, and not as the result of blind evolution. Institutions do not ordinarily just develop, but are deliberately created.

If the special position of the bishop of Rome, however, had simply developed from the fact that Rome was the capital city, his eminence would have been of a different kind. In this hypothesis, the bishop of Rome would have become a miniature emperor and the administrative element would have been prominent in his government of the Church. But in Christian antiquity there is no trace of a central administration conducting ecclesiastical affairs. The early popes were not heads of a bureaucracy, as the emperors had become.

Also, the prestige of the bishops of Constantinople, from the fourth century on, was due in part to the fact that Constantinople had become the imperial capital. But their position in the universal Church was notably different from that of the bishop of Rome. In Constantinople the bishop was the head and apex of the pyramid of ecclesiastical hierarchy, just as the emperor was over the civil hierarchy. But the bishop of Constantinople was never considered to be the focal point and source of vitality in the sacramental unity of the *communio*.

Finally, the personal element always played a subordinate role in the history of the Roman primacy. One has to trace the list of the popes down to St. Leo the Great (died 461) before a really towering figure emerges. None of the Roman bishops can really be compared with their contemporaries in the episcopate like Ignatius of Antioch, Polycarp, Irenaeus, Cyprian, Dionysius of Alexandria, Athanasius, Basil, John Chrysostom, or Augustine.

Therefore, if we are to give any explanation of the historical phenomenon of Rome's preeminence in the early Church, there is nothing left but to affirm that it was rooted in the nature of the Church itself. In some way the privileged position of the Apostle Peter, and his function as the rock, must have passed to the bishops of Rome. This is the one hypothesis that makes intelligible how the church of Rome became the focal point in the *communio,* from which "the rights of the treasured *communio*" (Ambrose) go forth into all the other churches.

THEOLOGY OF THE PRIMACY

The more the historical data forces us to recognize the actual preeminence of the bishop of Rome among the other bishops of the early Church, the more surprising it is that this very fundamental aspect of the Church was so little discussed by the earliest theological writers. If we consult the traditional pre-Nicene texts witnessing to the Roman primacy, we find texts speaking of Peter, of his sojourn in Rome, and of his martyrdom; the list of the popes compiled by Irenaeus; historical notes on the Easter controversy; and Hippolytus' words about Callistus. In all this, however, there is no theoretical discussion of the primacy of the Roman bishop. The only writing that even treats the theology of the Church is Cyprian's work, *The Unity of the Catholic Church.*

This treatise speaks extensively of the primacy of Peter, and the unity of the Church is traced to Peter's function as the rock. But the bishop of Rome is never mentioned. One inevitably asks how it was possible for a theologian to write even so short a treatise on the Catholic Church without once mentioning the pope. C. A. Kellner long ago pointed out that Cyprian's work is a polemical treatise dealing primarily with the Novatian schism. In a time of controversy over just who was the legitimate pope, Cyprian could hardly use communion with the pope as the touchstone of the legitimacy of the other bishops.[102] Even if this were an adequate solution, our question remains unanswered. How was it that for centuries no theologian made a clear and unmistakable statement that the bishop of Rome was the true and rightful head of the whole Catholic Church?

The scholarly Nicholas Cardinal Marini did exhaustive research on the doctrine of the primacy in the thought of St. John Chrysostom and came to the conclusion that Chrysostom undoubtedly taught a true primacy of the Apostle Peter.[103] But in no place does Chrysostom state that this primacy passed on to specific successors. Chrysostom does not deny this, and from his premises one can easily conclude that this must be the case. Chrysostom himself, however, does not draw this conclusion. The one passage that might possibly refer to the primacy comes in his treatise on the priesthood: "Why did Christ shed his blood? To redeem the flock which he entrusted to Peter and to his successors."[104] But the successors or, as Chrysostom puts it, those "after him," could be all the bishops. He does not say that they are the Roman bishops.

How was such a thing possible at the end of the fourth century, when the claims of the Roman bishop to a primacy—and the actual exercise of some kind of primacy—were well known? How could one writing at this time and even remotely dealing with Peter and the question of jurisdiction in the Church pass over this fundamental question in silence? Chrysostom, it seems, could hardly avoid taking some kind of stand either for or against it.

In resolving this question we must guard against the error into which so many historians fall. In fact, those who speak most of development often seem least capable of imagining any stage in theological history short of that of complete development.

What occurred here in the theology of the primacy can be observed as well in almost all areas of Catholic doctrine. Individual elements of a truth can be clearly traced back to the remotest times, but we see that it took long centuries for these elements to be brought together and formulated in propositions and abstract theses. Theological elaboration of the traditional faith was carried on very unevenly. The earliest theology dealt almost exclusively with trinitarian and christological doctrine. In the fourth century questions were raised about original sin, the redemption, and grace. Argument and speculation followed, and the result was a new formulation of these saving truths. A still longer time elapsed before a theology of the sacraments developed. In Christian antiquity and in the early Middle Ages, baptism, penance, the Eucharist, and holy orders played an impor- tant part in the lives of Christians, but these rites did not even bear the collective name "sacraments." We can trace belief in the real presence of Christ in the Eucharist back to the earliest times, but a thousand years went by before the concept of transubstantiation was forged. Theological reflection on the nature of the Church, on its teaching office and organization, developed still later; parts of it came only at the Council of Trent in the sixteenth century. None- theless, during this whole era there was a living Church that was organized and actually teaching. This Church, furthermore, was an object of faith, as we know from the creeds that affirm among their fundamental articles "the one, holy, and apostolic Church."

Therefore we should not be surprised that we do not possess a theological treatise on "The Church and the Primacy" from the third or even the sixth or ninth century. Neither do we have a treatise entitled "Sacramental Principles." The whole theological framework for such a treatise on the Church was missing. This does not mean, though, that the individual elements were not known or believed. If we did possess a list of commonly held ecclesiological theses from the second or third century, it would look something like the following:

1 There is only one true Church and outside it one cannot be saved.
2 The principal characteristic by which the true Church is recognized is the unity of the *communio*.
3 By Christ's command, Peter was the head of the apostles and the unity of the Church originates from him.
4 The deposit of faith is in later times preserved intact in the churches founded by the apostles, especially in the church of Rome.
5 The present bishop of Rome is the successor of the Apostle Peter.
6 *Communio* with the church of Rome is decisive for membership in the Church.

These theses, however, would not have been linked together or even considered to be integral parts of a theological treatise or system. The last two especially would not have been understood as theological propositions, but simply as statements of fact. The conclusion Catholics would naturally draw from these premises—that the Roman bishop has a primacy of teaching and jurisdiction over the whole Church—was not discussed as a theological question and so was never contested on this level. Our conclusion is that the elements of the later theology of the primacy and of its later exercise were present in the earliest years of the Church, but as dispersed fragments upon which one simply did not reflect. Therefore they were not linked in a theological system—which was exactly the situation in most of the other areas of theological teaching at that time.

Here there need be no argument from silence. There is silence about a systematic theological structure but not about the individual elements that are the foundation of the later structure. Neither is there silence about the application of these elements to the practical life of the Church.

Communio AND THE PRIMACY

Anyone who has dealt with the ancient sources would probably agree with our description of the *communio* and the position of Rome as its focal point. But the real question is still to be asked, and it is here that opinions differ sharply. Is this central position of the Roman bishops in the Church in fact an earlier form of the papal primacy as later understood in canon law and dogma? Is it not at most a germ from which in the course of time the later primacy could grow? Or is it not like a tree onto which so many alien branches have been grafted that it comes to bear fruits not anticipated in the original seed? St. Ambrose affirms that "the rights of the treasured *communio*" flowed forth from the Roman church to all the other churches. Let us grant that this was a common opinion. We know that the bishop of Rome, Damasus, had at that time a lively correspondence with the other churches. Jerome related that while he was in Rome Damasus commissioned him to answer questions posed by both eastern and western synods.

But can one really say that Damasus was ruling the whole Church in the manner of later popes?

Let us once more recall the premises. The early Church did not consist merely of a collection of bishops sharing the same attitudes. It was not just the arithmetical sum of all believers, but a multitude firmly bound together by the tie of a sacramental-juridical *communio*. Strictly speaking, this *communio* is what constitutes the *Una Sancta*, the one and holy Church. The focal point of the *communio* is the church of Rome along with its bishop. But since the *communio* is a sacramental-juridical structure, its center and focal point has a truly sacral authority. One excluded from the *communio* by the Roman bishop is no longer a member of the Church, and one whom he admits to communion becomes thereby a member of the Church. Each local bishop can also grant or refuse *communio*, but only so far as he speaks for the universal Church. Therefore he himself must be in communion with the Church, ultimately with the Roman church at the center of the *communio*. The bishop of Rome, however, does not need to derive his power from his communion with others, since he is himself the originating source of the whole. This is precisely what is meant by the fullness of papal power. It is exactly what our Lord conferred on Peter, when he used the completely apt metaphor of the keys of the kingdom of heaven.

Paradoxical as it may seem, the basic function of the pope in the Church is not his performance of certain official actions, but simply that he be present. Although we hear often of the bark guided by Peter at the helm, Christ's own image was of another kind, when he spoke of the rock on

71

which the Church is built. Here it is the pope who gives the Church its unity and makes it a living organism. Without him it would be simply an aggregation of people who share a common mentality. True, these equals could create an organization and choose a president. But this would be something quite different from the historical Church. It is not Peter who is built upon the Church, but the Church upon Peter. Primarily, this is a static role. To be the unifying principle of the Church, the pope need not perform official action. Still, he is not a lifeless rock or an abstract principle of unity. To belong to him, to be incorporated into the organism, depends on his will. And this is what is indicated by the metaphor of the keys of the kingdom.

The possibility of taking juridical action is therefore a derived consequence—although a necessary one—from the authority of the rock. If the pope holds the keys to the whole, and if it depends upon him who shall and who shall not be in the *communio*, then he can set conditions of communion and exclusion. He can even issue orders concerning matters of lesser importance in the affairs of the Church. But his authority is not exclusively shown in giving orders. He is not simply the superior of the bishops and the faithful in the way a general is over his officers and soldiers.

The position of the pope is still best described—although still imperfectly—by the analogy of the head and the members. The image is flawed, in that an organism manifests reciprocal interaction, with the members depending for life on the head and the head depending on the members. But the center of the *communio* does not owe his focal position to the other members of the *com-*

72

munio. His position has not been granted him by the members, it does not depend upon their cooperation, and they cannot take it away from him. Still, the image of the organism is right in showing the kind of authority exercised by the head. One can say that in the organism the head gives orders to the members, but the life of the whole is much more than simply the issuing and receiving of commands. The head and the members act as a single unit. Normally, orders—commands given in the face of opposition—are not given in the organism. In fact, only in the extraordinary case when differences arise do we think of the head and the members as distinct factors in the organism. Similarly, we should not look for the authority of the Roman bishops only in those cases in which he acts against opposition. Many years may pass without this being needed, but he still remains the focal point and juridical center from which the rights of the *communio* flow into all the other churches.

Moreover, the Roman bishops of the first centuries did not function simply as static principles of unity without ever performing acts of government. In fact, the first tangible event in the history of the Church after the death of the Apostle Peter is the letter in which Clement, bishop of Rome, intervened in the affairs of the church of Corinth. Possibly at this time the bishop of Smyrna could have intervened in Corinth with equal success; but then again it cannot be purely accidental that the bishop of Rome always did the things that other bishops, perhaps, could also have done.

At least from the second century onward, people in all quarters noted carefully the attitude of the bishop of Rome in questions of faith and discipline. Foreign theologians

73

came to Rome to learn and gain disciples there. The bishop of Smyrna came to Rome to win its bishop's support for the Asian way of dating Easter. The church of Lyons asked the bishop of Rome to judge the Montanists favorably, but Praxeas came from Asia Minor to argue for a negative judgment. With respect to all these persons and movements, Rome's bishop did not act as a theologian or a teacher, but as a judge. He excommunicated a whole series of teachers of heretical systems and doctrines. To counter Marcion's attempt to do away with half the books in the canon of Scripture, the church at Rome drafted what was probably an official index of the canonical books, as preserved in the so-called Muratorian Fragment.[105] The views of the bishop of Smyrna on the date of Easter were rebuffed. Admittedly, in any of these instances it cannot be shown that other bishops could not have performed similar acts. When the bishop of Rome expelled the presbyters Florinus and Blastus from his presbyterate during the second century because of heresy, this was no more than any other bishop could have done. But the total number of cases involving action from Rome is far greater than that for any other bishop or church. Our historical study must keep to what in fact did happen, and not to what perhaps could have happened.

In dealing with the Easter controversy, Pope Victor ordered that synods be held concurrently throughout the whole world and he was ready to expel an entire province from the *communio* because of its opposition—a measure unheard of in those times. His action stirred discontent in many places, but no one questioned his right to act as he did. Even this case can be judged in different ways, but one

74

cannot eventually avoid the question whether the exponent of such authority can be called anything else but the head of the Church.

In the dispute over reconciling persons guilty of the unpardonable sins, the attitude of Popes Callistus and Cornelius was in the end, without any formal legislation, decisive for the practice and teaching of the whole Church despite vigorous resistance from many sides. The same procedure was repeated in the controversy over the validity of heretical baptism. On other occasions we find the bishop of Rome excluding whole provinces from the *communio* for opposing him, without his own position being in any way shaken. Pope Stephen intervened authoritatively and effectively when there were disturbances in the Spanish church, while refusing to intervene in a similar situation in the church of Gaul, although much pressure was put on him to do so. These two cases are also open to different interpretations—with this one exception, namely, that Stephen was less than certain about his own authority and rights.[106]

Pope Dionysius required Dionysius of Alexandria, bishop of the most important episcopal see of the East, to answer charges that he was teaching dangerous doctrine. And the bishop of Alexandria proved very eager to defend himself before the pope. Earlier, the greatest living theologian of the time, Origen of Alexandria, came before Pope Fabian with the same eagerness. Here, too, one can construct hypothetical cases in which other bishops might have taken similar action. If Cyprian, bishop of Carthage, had criticized the teaching of the bishop of Antioch, for example, the latter might well have replied to him just as Dionysius of Alexandria replied to Pope Dionysius, but this would not have led to the conclusion that Cyprian had a primacy over the whole Church. It can be no accident that such acts, which could conceivably have occurred elsewhere, were actually repeated frequently in Rome.

One might also invert the question and ask just what the earliest bishops of Rome should have done to show future historians more clearly that they were heads of the Church? Dispute more, command more, issue more general regulations, excommunicate more people, install and depose more bishops? Certainly, the list of such actions that the Roman bishops undertook in the first three centuries outside their local area is not very long, and some of these acts were no more than any other important bishop could have undertaken—such as sending alms to Arabia, Corinth, or Cappadocia. But one must ask whether the picture would be any different if the list were longer. For even the little we do know is enough to show that the bishops of Rome occupied a position of real preeminence, even in the juridical sphere. They were well aware of their position in the Catholic *communio* and the other bishops accepted this as a matter of course.

NOTES

The following abbreviations are used in the notes.

CSEL—*Corpus Scriptorum Ecclesiasticorum Latinorum*
NCE—*New Catholic Encyclopedia*
  PG—*Patrologia Graeca*
  PL—*Patrologia Latina*

1 *The Unity of the Church Against the Donatists*, 20, 56. PL 43, 434.
2 *Against Cresconius*, III, 35, 39. PL 43, 517.
3 *The Donatist Schism*, II, 13. PL 11, 965.
4 TRANSLATOR'S NOTE: It is disputed whether the earliest Christian uses of the phrase *communio sanctorum* refer to "common life with the saints" (*sancti*), that is, with the confessors, martyrs, and baptized faithful, or to "common sharing in holy things" (*sancta*), that is, in faith and the sacraments, especially the Eucharist. J. N. D. Kelly, *Early Christian Creeds* (London: Longmans, Green, 1950), pp. 388-97; W. Elert, *Eucharist and Church Fellowship in the First Four Centuries* (St. Louis: Concordia, 1966), pp. 9-21, 204-23; F. X. Lawlor, art. "Communion of Saints," NCE 4, 41-43; W. Breuning, art. "Communion of Saints," *Sacramentum Mundi* 1, 391-94.
5 Given among the letters of St. Jerome, Letter 92. PL 22, 764.

6 Found in Hefele, *Conciliengeschichte* II (Freiburg, 1875), 62.

7 *De symbolo*, 10. Given by F. J. Badcock, "*Sanctorum communio* as an Article in the Creed," *Journal of Theological Studies* 21 (1920), 110.

8 *The Prescription of Heretics*, 32. PL 2, 45.

9 Given among the letters of St. Jerome, Letter 131. PL 22, 1125.

10 In the original: *quiescit in pace, depositus in pace, vixit in pace, pax tibi cum sanctis, vale in pace.*

11 *Dormit in pace, Anima dulcis in pace bene quiescas.*

12 *Vixit in pace, Obiit in pace, Resurrecturus in pace.*

13 G. DeRossi, *Inscriptiones christianae urbis Romae*, n. 132.

14 E. Diehl, *Inscriptiones Latinae Christianae Veteres*, n. 1579A; I, 303.

15 *History of the Arians*, 28. PG 25, 725.

16 *Apology Against the Arians*, 20. PG 25, 281.

17 *Encyclical Epistle to the Bishops Throughout the World*, 2. PG 25, 225.

18 Epistle to the Philadelphians, 11; Epistle to the Smyrneans, 12. *The Apostolic Fathers*, ed. J. B. Lightfoot, 1, 127 and 130.

19 Letter XII, to Gratian, 4. PL 16, 988 f.

20 Letter 72, 3. CSEL III/2, 778.

21 TRANSLATOR'S NOTE: In the second century the churches of Syria and Asia Minor celebrated Easter on the day of the Jewish Passover, the 14th of Nisan (*die quarta decima*, hence the name "Quartodecimans"). The Roman practice emphasized Christianity's break from Judaism by always celebrating Easter on a Sunday. Pope Victor (189-198) was especially concerned to bring about uniformity of practice and proposed excommunicating the Asian Quartodeciman bishops. Jules Lebreton and Jacques Zeiller, *History of the Primitive Church* III (London: Burns, Oates, 1946), 589-93; Karl Baus, *From the Apostolic Community to Constantine*, Vol. I of *Handbook of Church History*, ed. H. Jedin (London: Burns and Oates, 1965), 268-72; J. Ford, art. "Easter Controversy," NCE 5, 8-9, and "Quartodeciman," NCE 12, 13.

22 Given by Eusebius, *Ecclesiastical History*, V, 24. PG 20, 508.

23 *Apostolic Constitutions*, II, 58, 3; ed. F. X. Funk (Paderborn, 1905), I, 168.

24 See Eusebius, *Ecclesiastical History*, V, 24. PG 20, 506 f.

25 Letter to Decentius, 5. PL 20, 557.

26 Letter 4, 5. PL 61, 167.

27 Socrates, *Ecclesiastical History*, II, 38. PG 47, 325.

28 *Encomium of Saints Cyrus and John*, 12. PG 87/3, 3460 f.

29 *The Spiritual Meadow*, 48. PG 87/3, 2904.

30 *Ecclesiastical History*, VIII, 5. PG 67, 1527.

31 *The Spiritual Meadow*, 30. PG 87/3, 2877.
32 Ibid., 29. PG 87/3, 2876.
33 Question 113. PG 89, 766.
34 *Encomium of Saints Cyrus and John*, 36. PG 87/3, 3553.
35 *Ecclesiastical History*, IV, 10. PG 82, 1144.
36 Given by Badcock, "Sanctorum communio," *Journal of Theological Studies* 21 (1920), 109.
37 *The Unity of the Catholic Church*, 17. CSEL III/1, 226.
38 In Latin: *litterae communicatoriae, litterae canonicae, commendatitiae.*
39 TRANSLATOR'S NOTE: In the early Church, chorbishops were bishops of people living in villages and in the country. They were eventually subordinated to metropolitan bishops with whom they served as auxiliaries over a region of his diocese. P. Joannou, art. "Chorbishop," NCE 3, 625 f.; James A. Mohler, *The Origin and Evolution of the Priesthood* (Staten Island, New York: Alba House, 1970), pp. 74-76.
40 Given by Mansi, *Sacrorum conciliorum . . . collectio* 2, 1131.
41 *Ecclesiastical History*, V, 16. PG 67, 1261.
42 Letter 44. CSEL XXXIV/2, 111.
43 *Against Praxeas*, 1. PL 2, 178.
44 Letter 59, 9. CSEL III/2, 676 f.
45 *Ecclesiastical History*, VI, 43. PG 20, 629.
46 *The Prescription of Heretics*, 20. PL 2, 37.
47 See the letter of the Roman presbyters and deacons, given among the letters of St. Cyprian, Letter 39. CSEL III/2, 575.
48 Letter 129, 3. PG 32, 561.
49 *The Donatist Schism*, II, 6. PL 11, 959.
50 Letter 204, 7. PG 32, 753 f.
51 Letter 191. PG 32, 704.
52 TRANSLATOR'S NOTE: The *lapsi* ("fallen") are those who apostatized from the faith during persecution. In the middle of the third century, controversy raged over the practice of granting them reconciliation and restoration to full communion after penance. The rigorist Novatian sect listed apostasy as one of the unforgivable sins. B. Poschmann, *Penance and the Anointing of the Sick* (New York: Herder and Herder, 1964), pp. 52-58; Baus, *From the Apostolic Community to Constantine*, pp. 318-45; F. Hauser, art. "Lapsi," NCE 8, 384.
53 Socrates, *Ecclesiastical History*, VI, 18. PG 67, 717.
54 Letter 41, 2. CSEL III/2, 588 f.
55 Letter 67, 3. CSEL III/2, 737.
56 Socrates, *Ecclesiastical History*, VI, 9. PG 67, 693.
57 Canon 13. Mansi, *Sacrorum consiliorum . . . collectio* 2, 971.
58 Letter 209, 5. CSEL LVII, 349 f.

59 TRANSLATOR'S NOTE: The Donatists were rigorist African Christians of the fourth and fifth centuries who claimed that bishops who had collaborated with imperial officials in time of persecution could no longer validly ordain. The Donatist schism took on a strongly ethnic and anti-Roman character and, arguing from texts of Cyprian, came to deny the validity of all sacraments conferred by sinful ministers. First St. Optatus of Milevis and then St. Augustine wrote in defense of the catholicity of the Church and of the objective validity of the sacraments. W. H. C. Frend, *The Donatist Church* (Oxford: Clarendon Press, 1952); G. C. Willis, *St. Augustine and the Donatists* (London: SPCK, 1950); S. L. Greenslade, *Schism in the Early Church* (London: SCM, ²1964); D. Faul, art. "Donatism," NCE 4, 1001-03.

60 Letter 188. PG 32, 664.

61 *The Donatist Schism*, III, 9. PL 11, 1020.

62 Ibid., I, 3. PL 11, 890.

63 *The Prescription of Heretics*, 5. PL 2, 20.

64 Given among St. Cyprian's letters, Letter 75, 24. CSEL III/2, 825.

65 Letter 129, 3. PG 32, 562.

66 Letter 14, 4. CSEL III/2, 512.

67 Given among St. Cyprian's letters, Letter 30, 5. CSEL III/2, 553.

68 *The Martyrdom of St. Polycarp. The Apostolic Fathers* 1, 189.

69 *The Letters and Other Remains of Dionysius of Alexandria*, ed. C. L. Feltoe (London: Cambridge University Press, 1904), compare p. 17, line 8, with p. 18, line 10.

70 Polybius, *Histories*, III, 22, 4. Loeb Classical Library edition, II, 54.

71 Epistle to the Philadelphians, 4. *The Apostolic Fathers* 1, 124.

72 Epistle to the Ephesians, 20. *The Apostolic Fathers* 1, 111.

73 Epistle to the Smyrneans, 8. *The Apostolic Fathers* 1, 129.

74 *Didache* (The Teaching of the Apostles), 9. *The Apostolic Fathers* 1, 221.

75 *Altkirchliche Autonomie und päpstlicher Zentralismus* (Munich: Reinhart, 1941), p. 16.

76 *The Donatist Schism*, II, 6. PL 11, 959.

77 See page 30 above.

78 *Against Cresconius*, II, 37, 46. PL 43, 494.

79 *Adversus Hereses*, III, 4, 1. PG 7, 855.

80 *The Prescription of Heretics*, 21. PL 2, 38.

81 *The Donatist Schism*, II, 3. PL 11, 949.

82 Letter 42, 3, 7. PL 33, 163.

83 Letter 14, 1. PL 20, 777.

84 *Geschichte des Papsttums* 1 (Tübingen: Mohr, 1930), 381.

85 Letter 11, 4. PL 16, 986.

86 Letter 15, 2. PL 22, 355.
87 Ibid.
88 Letter 48, 3. CSEL III/2, 607.
89 Letter 59, 14. CSEL III/2, 683.
90 *Against Praxeas*, 1. PL 2, 178.
91 *Adversus Hereses*, III, 3, 2. PG 7, 849.
92 Karl Bihlmeyer and Hermann Tüchle, *Church History* 1 (Westminster, Maryland: Newman Press, 1958), 115 f.
93 "*Prokathemene tes agapes*," Epistle to the Romans, 1. *The Apostolic Fathers* 1, 120.
94 *Ecclesiastical History*, VII, 30. PG 20, 720.
95 *Apology Against the Arians*, 20. PG 25, 281.
96 *Geschichte des Papsttums* 1, 72-83.
97 *On Purity*, 21. PL 2, 1079. TRANSLATOR'S NOTE: See the extended comment on this phrase by W. L. Le Saint, S. J., in the Ancient Christian Writers edition, *Tertullian—Treatises on Penance* (Westminster, Maryland: Newman Press, 1959), pp. 284-86.
98 Letter 59, 14. CSEL III/2, 683.
99 TRANSLATOR'S NOTE: In North Africa and Asia Minor in the third century, baptism performed by heretics was generally regarded as invalid. But in Rome such baptisms were judged valid, and persons baptized in heresy were reconciled with the Church simply by absolution. Synodal decrees of African local councils and a treatise by St. Cyprian were directed against the Roman practice. Pope Stephen rejected the African contention and imposed the tradition prevailing in Rome. E. G. Weltin, art. "Stephen I, Pope, St.," NCE 13, 694; Baus, *From the Apostolic Community to Constantine*, pp. 360-65.
100 See Firmilian's letter, given among the letters of St. Cyprian, Letter 75, 17. CSEL III/2, 821.
101 "Neue Untersuchungen über die Ursprünge der kirchlichen Primatslehre," *Tübingen theologische Quartalschrift* 109 (1928), 256.
102 C. A. Kellner, S. J., "Cyprians Schrift von der Einheit der Kirche," *Zeitschrift für katholische Theologie* 36 (1912), 288.
103 *Il primato di S. Pietro et de' suoi successori in San Giovanni Crisostomo* (Rome: Tipografico pontificia Artigianelli, 1919).
104 *The Priesthood*, II, 1. PG 48, 632.
105 TRANSLATOR'S NOTE: Marcion was a Gnostic from Asia Minor whose rigorist teaching became widespread during the second century. He held that the Old Testament could have no place in Christianity, since its God of creation and retribution stood in complete contrast to the God of mercy and love revealed by Jesus. In the New Testament, Marcion accepted only an expurgated version of Luke and ten

epistles. The orthodox reaction to the Marcionite movement included the drafting of a canon of the accepted biblical books, of which the oldest extant example was discovered by L. A. Muratori in 1740. Hans Jonas, *The Gnostic Religion* (Boston: Beacon Press, 1958), pp. 137-46; A. A. Stephenson, art. "Marcion," NCE 9, 193-94; W. G. Most, art. "Muratorian Canon," NCE 10, 81-82.

106 G. Bardy, "L'autorite de siège Romain et les controverses du IIIe Siècle," *Recherches de Science Religieuse* 14 (1924), 389 f.

INDEX

Damasus, pope, 55, 57, 70, 71
Decius, emperor, 42
DeRossi, G., 78
Diehl, E., 78
Dionysius, bishop of Alexandria, 31, 32, 41, 44, 65, 75
Dionysius of Corinth, 44
Dionysius, pope, 75

Elert, Werner, 4, 77
Eleutherius, pope, 33
Eusebius, 60, 61, 78
Eustathius, bishop of Sebaste, 37

Fabian, pope, 34, 35, 75
Fabius, bishop of Antioch, 31, 34, 44
Faul, D., 80
Felicissimus, 36, 37
Felix II (antipope), 20
Feltoe, C. L., 80
Firmilian, 41, 63, 81
Florinus, presbyter of Rome, 74
Ford, J., 78
Frend, W. H. C., 80
Funk, F. X., 78

Gratian, emperor, 57
Greenslade, S. L., 80
Gregory Thaumaturgus, St., 38

Hamer, Jerome, 4
Hauser, F., 79
Hefele, C. J., 78
Hegesippus, 62
Heiler, Friedrich, 48
Helidorus, bishop of Laodicea, 32
Heracleon, 62
Hertling, Ludwig, 2, 3, 4, 5, 6, 7, 8, 10, 11, 12, 13, 14
Hippolytus, 66

Ignatius of Antioch, St., 3, 21, 43, 44, 46, 51, 60, 65
Innocent I, pope, 24, 25
Irenaeus, St., 3, 23, 24, 44, 55, 59, 60, 65, 66
Iserloh, Erwin, 14
Isidore (monk), 38

James of Viterbo, 1
James, St., 54
Jedin, H., 78
Jerome, St., 19, 57, 58, 70, 77, 78
Joannou, P., 79
John Chrysostom, St., 26, 37, 38, 65, 67
John Moschus, 26, 27
Jonas, Hans, 82
Jonathan, high priest, 45
Julian the Apostate, 29
Julius, pope, 21, 61
Justin, 62

Kellner, C. A., 66, 81
Kelly, J. N. D., 77
Küng, Hans, 11

Lawlor, F. X., 77
Lebreton, Jules, 78
Le Guillou, M.-J., 4
Leo the Great, St., 65
Le Saint, W. L., 81
Liberius, pope, 20
Lightfoot, J. B., 78
Loretz, Philip, 14

McCue, James F., 3
Macedonius, patriarch of Constantinople, 25, 37
Mansi, G. D., 79
Marcellus, bishop of Ancyra, 61
Marcion, 36, 40, 62, 74, 81
Marini, Nicholas Cardinal, 67

Martin of Tours, St., 39
Matthew, St., 63
Maximilla, 32
Mazabanes, bishop of Jerusalem, 32
Meletius, bishop of Antioch, 42, 58
Mohler, James A., 4, 79
Montanus, 32, 33, 40, 59, 74
Mörsdorf, K., 8
Most, W. G., 82
Muratori, L. A., 82
Murray, Robert, 14

Nicetas of Remesiana, 17
Nimes, Council of, 17
Novatian, 31, 34, 37, 40, 66, 79

Onias, high priest, 45
Optatus of Milevis, 16, 35, 40, 53, 55, 56, 80
Origen, 62, 75

Paul of Samosata, 60
Paul, St., 50, 51, 54, 59, 64
Paulinus, bishop of Antioch, 42, 58
Paulinus of Nola, St., 25
Peter, archpresbyter, 38
Peter, St., 3, 63, 64, 65, 66, 67, 69, 71, 72, 73
Polybius, 80
Polycarp of Smyrna, 23, 43, 44, 51, 65
Poschmann, B., 79
Praxeas, 32, 33, 59, 62, 74
Prisca, 32
Privatus of Lambesis, 34
Proclus, 62

Quintianus, 20

Rahner, Karl, 8
Ratzinger, Joseph, 4, 14
Ryan, Seamus, 9

Siricius, pope, 55
Smothers, Edgar R., 3
Socrates, 78, 79
Sophronius, 25, 26
Soter, pope, 33
Sozomen, 26, 29
Stephen, pope, 31, 32, 41, 63, 75, 81
Stephenson, A. A., 82
Suenens, Cardinal, 8, 11

Tatian, 62
Tertullian, 19, 32, 33, 34, 40, 51, 55, 59, 63
Thelymides, bishop of Laodicea, 32
Theodoret, 27
Theodotus the Elder, 62
Theodotus the Younger, 62
Theophilus of Alexandria, 16, 38
Torquemada, Juan, 1
Tüchle, Hermann, 81

Valentinian, emperor, 57
Valentinus, 36, 40, 62
Victor, pope, 33, 44, 52, 74, 78
Vitalis, bishop of Antioch, 58

Weltin, E. G., 81
Willis, G. C., 80

Zeiller, Jacques, 78
Zephyrinus, pope, 32

About this book
Communio: Church and Papacy in Early Christianity was set in the composing room of Loyola University Press. The typeface is 12/15, 11/13, and 9/11 Caledonia.

It was printed by Photopress, Inc., on Warren's 60-pound English Finish paper and bound by The Engdahl Company.